IMAGES
of America

BOSTON YOUTH
SYMPHONY ORCHESTRAS

Federico Cortese, who became the music director of the Boston Youth Symphony Orchestras in 1999, conducts a concert at Boston's Symphony Hall.

On the cover: The Boston Youth Symphony Orchestras' debut concert took place on May 10, 1959, at New England Conservatory's Jordan Hall. This photograph, showing the orchestra onstage before the performance, appeared on a postcard printed by the organization following the completion of its first season. (Courtesy of the Boston Youth Symphony Orchestras.)

IMAGES
of America

BOSTON YOUTH
SYMPHONY ORCHESTRAS

Krysten A. Keches

ARCADIA
PUBLISHING

Published by Arcadia Publishing
Charleston SC, Chicago IL, Portsmouth NH, San Francisco CA

Library of Congress Catalog Card Number: 2007930475

For all general information contact Arcadia Publishing at:
Telephone 843-853-2070
Fax 843-853-0044
E-mail sales@arcadiapublishing.com
For customer service and orders:
Toll-Free 1-888-313-2665

Visit us on the Internet at www.arcadiapublishing.com

This book is dedicated to the thousands of young musicians that the Boston Youth Symphony Orchestras has served over the course of its history. During their time in the Boston Youth Symphony Orchestras, children from throughout New England have engaged in a collective celebration of the classical music tradition through their inspiring dedication and with their remarkable talent.

CONTENTS

ACKNOWLEDGMENTS

The Boston Youth Symphony Orchestras would like to acknowledge the dedicated work of Dr. Marvin Rabin. As the founding music director of the organization, he played an integral role in the development of the program and goals of the Boston Youth Symphony Orchestras. Rabin's 1968 dissertation, a history and analysis of the organization from 1958 to 1964, demonstrates the passionate commitment to music education that he has exemplified throughout his life. Written at the University of Illinois, his dissertation also served as a valuable resource for this retrospective. Rabin's ideas continue to resonate today, and the Boston Youth Symphony Orchestras thanks him for bringing the organization to life.

INTRODUCTION

In 1958, Dr. Robert Choate, then chairman of the Division of Music at Boston University's School of Fine and Applied Arts (now the College of Fine Arts), led the university's effort to establish a youth orchestra for junior and senior high school students. Since its inception, the Boston Youth Symphony Orchestras (BYSO), formerly known as the Greater Boston Youth Symphony Orchestras, has served thousands of young musicians from throughout New England. Over the past 50 years, the BYSO has evolved from a single orchestra to one of Boston's most prestigious arts organizations, with a range of programs that includes three full symphonic orchestras, a string orchestra, a preparatory wind ensemble, four chamber orchestras, 50 chamber music ensembles, and a nationally recognized string training program for underrepresented youth from inner-city communities.

As the first music director of the BYSO, Dr. Marvin Rabin worked to expand the organization, foster musical distinction, and reach out to the Greater Boston community. By 1969, under the direction of Dr. Walter Eisenberg, the BYSO had organized its first international tour of Switzerland; since then, members of the orchestras have traveled to perform at venues throughout Europe, Asia, South America, and the Middle East. Other highlights from the BYSO's history include concerts at Carnegie Hall, the White House, and annual performances at some of the finest venues in the New England area.

Federico Cortese assumed the post of music director in 1999 and is the conductor of the BYSO's most accomplished ensemble, the Boston Youth Symphony. During his tenure, Cortese has instituted several significant initiatives that have advanced the organization artistically. Today the BYSO has the largest operating budget of any youth orchestra in the United States, nearly double that of most youth orchestras, which reflects the organization's programmatic scope and commitment to artistic excellence.

In March 2007, the Greater Boston Youth Symphony Orchestras officially became the Boston Youth Symphony Orchestras. In this retrospective, the name Greater Boston Youth Symphony Orchestra (GBYSO) refers to the original single orchestra, which is now known as the Boston Youth Symphony. Throughout the book, the name BYSO refers to the organization as a whole.

Dedicated to providing talented young musicians with opportunities for personal and artistic growth, the BYSO is widely regarded as one of the country's finest youth orchestras and is recognized nationally as a model music and arts education organization. The BYSO invites all to be part of the musical legacy and future plans that continue to make the BYSO one of the finest cultural institutions in the country.

One

FROM 1958 TO 1969

Following its establishment in 1958, the Boston Youth Symphony Orchestras (BYSO) flourished under the leadership of music director Dr. Marvin Rabin. One hundred and thirty-five students auditioned for membership in the original single ensemble, attesting to the need for an orchestral program for high school–age musicians in the Boston area. Throughout the next decade, the orchestra performed at major concert venues, including Boston's Symphony Hall, New England Conservatory's Jordan Hall, and Harvard University's Sanders Theatre. The orchestra also appeared at local schools, bringing classical music to younger audiences in the community. By 1969, the BYSO had performed at both Carnegie Hall and the White House and had undertaken its first international tour; these early accomplishments helped to ensure the growth of the organization in the years to come.

An associate professor of music at Boston University from 1958 to 1966, the BYSO's founding music director, Dr. Marvin Rabin, led the orchestra for six seasons, until 1964. Under his guidance, the orchestra thrived, gradually increasing its membership and gaining recognition within the Greater Boston community. Thanks to his dedication, the BYSO flourished in its early years.

Rabin worked to raise the caliber of the orchestra, expand its repertoire, and spread enthusiasm about classical music by strengthening the link between the BYSO and local schools. Through his efforts, he established many of the goals and traditions that remain vital to the organization today.

The final selection of members for the opening season was completed in January 1959; 135 students auditioned and 80 were accepted into the orchestra. Rehearsals were held on Saturday mornings from 9:30 until noon at what is now called the College of Fine Arts Concert Hall at Boston University, the same space where members of the Boston Youth Symphony practice today. Here members of the brass section of the Greater Boston Youth Symphony Orchestra (GBYSO) rehearse together around 1959.

GBYSO's first concert took place on May 1, 1959, at Wayland High School and served as a warm-up for the orchestra's debut performance on May 10, 1959, at New England Conservatory's Jordan Hall. The program, titled "Salute to UNICEF," included works by Max Bruch, Alan Hovhaness, and Richard Wagner, as well as the premiere of Concert Overture No. 1, a piece written specifically for GBYSO by the young composer Jerome Cohen.

THE
GREATER BOSTON YOUTH
SYMPHONY ORCHESTRA

MARVIN RABIN, Conductor

presents

SALUTE TO UNICEF

JORDAN HALL, BOSTON
SUNDAY, MAY 10, 1959
3.30 P.M.

PRINTED BY INDUSTRIAL SCHOOL FOR CRIPPLED CHILDREN

SEAL DESIGNED BY JUDITH DUDDY, MARBLEHEAD HIGH SCHOOL

After a successful first year, the BYSO completed auditions for its second season in October 1959; 98 students were accepted into the orchestra, an increase of 18 members. The 1959–1960 season marked the initiation of concerts for children; these annual performances emphasized the goal of spreading classical music to young audiences.

On January 17, 1960, GBYSO performed at Harvard University's Sanders Theatre in honor of the 85th birthday of Nobel Peace Prize winner Albert Schweitzer. The program included works by Johann Sebastian Bach, Gabriel Fauré, Aaron Copland, Alan Hovhaness, and Alexander Borodin. Violinist Daniel Kobialka (class of 1961), the concertmaster of the orchestra, performed Introduction and Rondo Capriccioso by Camille Saint-Saëns.

One of the highlights of the second season was the taping of an educational video for Channel 2 at the Massachusetts Institute of Technology on January 30, 1960. Intended as a teaching tool for elementary and junior high school–age audiences, the program was used in New England area classrooms and for National Educational Television. The first video in a series of programs titled *Accent on Music*, the tape showed the orchestra in rehearsal at the Massachusetts Institute of Technology's Kresge Auditorium. The program used the contemporary manuscript "Dance Mosaics" by Kenneth Wright to introduce the characteristics of individual instruments, and violin soloist Daniel Kobialka (class of 1961) performed Introduction and Rondo Capriccioso by Saint-Saëns.

Second Annual Concert
THE GREATER BOSTON YOUTH SYMPHONY ORCHESTRA
MARVIN RABIN, Conductor
JORDAN HALL, BOSTON   MAY 8, 1960

GBYSO performed nine concerts in total during the 1959–1960 season; in fact, the orchestra received more invitations to perform than could be accepted. The second annual concert at New England Conservatory's Jordan Hall took place on May 8, 1960, and included Aaron Copland's "Fanfare for the Common Man," the first movement of Alexander Borodin's Symphony No. 2, Georges Bizet's L'Arlesienne Suite No. 2, and Bedrich Smetana's "Dance of the Comedians" from *The Bartered Bride*. The program notes stated that the goals of the organization were "to provide a broader musical challenge and opportunity for talented junior and senior high school students, to contribute to the schools and communities from which they come, to play for a larger audience and especially for other young people."

At the beginning of the BYSO's third season, the number of students auditioning for the orchestra jumped to 300, evidence of the growing esteem for the organization. With members highly committed to the study of classical music, the orchestra was better able to meet the demands of more standard symphonic repertoire and presented 12 concerts between 1960 and 1961. Cellist Jeanne Wilson Bateman (class of 1961), pictured here, was a member of GBYSO for three seasons.

The "Friends of Music" of Niskayuna Public Schools

Present

The Greater Boston
Youth Symphony Orchestra

MARVIN RABIN
Conductor

The third season included appearances at local schools, the continuation of children's concerts, and an overnight trip to perform in Niskayuna, New York. The third annual concert at New England Conservatory's Jordan Hall took place on March 26, 1961, and included Nikolai Rimsky-Korsakov's *Russian Easter Overture* and Pyotr Ilich Tchaikovsky's *Swan Lake*.

On April 23, 1961, GBYSO had the honor of performing at world-renowned Carnegie Hall. Alongside the Pilgrim Fellowship Choir of the Manhasset Congregational Church in Long Island, GBYSO performed works by Guiseppe Verdi, Jean Sibelius, and Richard Wagner. Both groups presented a second concert one week later at New England Conservatory's Jordan Hall.

At Carnegie Hall, the orchestra also gave the premiere of "Give Me the Splendid, Silent Sun," a piece by Normand Lockwood set to text by Walt Whitman. In recognition of the orchestra's trip to New York, Gov. John A. Volpe named April 23 Greater Boston Youth Symphony Day in the commonwealth of Massachusetts.

16

On May 20, 1961, Arthur Fiedler, then conductor of the Boston Pops Orchestra, led GBYSO in a rehearsal of *Die Meistersinger von Nürnberg* as part of a music education clinic sponsored by John Coffey, a trombonist in the Boston Symphony Orchestra. The appearance also marked the first time that a large audience of music educators had heard the orchestra.

In August 1961, at the beginning of the BYSO's fourth season, the members of the orchestra participated in a one-week summer workshop at Sargent Camp in Peterborough, New Hampshire. Owned by Boston University, the 1,000-acre lakeside property served as an ideal location for the young musicians to begin working on the repertoire for the upcoming season.

During the summer workshop, 13 music coaches, 7 of which were members of the Boston Symphony Orchestra, led sectional rehearsals, chamber music groups, sight-reading sessions, and conducting classes. One of the main objectives of the workshop was to familiarize the orchestra with a wide range of orchestral repertoire and chamber music. Sight-reading sessions in the evenings allowed the musicians to tackle difficult literature, and by the end of the week, the students had read about 40 complete works. In addition to practicing required pieces, students were able to check out music taken to camp from the BYSO's collection and from the newly inventoried Boston University music library. Here clarinet coach Felix Viscuglia instructs, from left to right, (second row) William Cabral (class of 1964), David Maslanka (class of 1961), Gerald Bowman (class of 1963), and John Rapoza (class of 1962); (first row) Nancy Gilmore (class of 1962), Judith Dietz (class of 1962), and Abigail Schirmer (class of 1961) during a sectional rehearsal.

With about seven hours each day devoted to rehearsals, the students received a great deal of individual attention from the music staff while at Sargent Camp. Here (from left to right) William Gordon Allen (class of 1963) and Robert Davidson (class of 1962) participate in a bassoon sectional during the workshop; small rehearsals such as this one took place twice every day.

The workshop also allowed the musicians and coaches to get to know one another. While regular weekly rehearsals left little free time for members of GBYSO to bond, the recreation periods built into the camp schedule gave the musicians the opportunity to relax by the lake, play sports, and even spontaneously form ensembles.

At the end of the workshop, GBYSO gave an informal afternoon concert at Sargent Camp for friends and family members. The performance included pieces by Wolfgang Amadeus Mozart, Antonín Dvořák, and Ralph Vaughan Williams, which the orchestra would continue to work on in the fall. The BYSO's first camp established a tradition that continues today as an integral part of each season.

During its fourth season, GBYSO was honored by an invitation to perform at the White House. The concert date was set for April 16, 1962, and a performance at Carnegie Hall for the United Nations was also contracted for later that week. The musicians traveled together by airplane to Washington, D.C., the day before the concert.

On April 16, 1962, GBYSO performed in an outdoor shell on the south lawn of the White House under the direction of its founding music director, Dr. Marvin Rabin. While waiting for the concert to begin, the young musicians tried to stay warm in the 40-degree weather. Once onstage, the orchestra played the traditional "Hail to the Chief" as the president and first lady walked to their seats.

Perched on the stage erected specifically for the concert, Rabin kneels to greet Jacqueline Kennedy. This photograph appeared on the front cover of the September 1962 issue of *Orchestra News*, a quarterly magazine that focused on the development of orchestras in the United States.

Pres. John F. Kennedy gave welcoming remarks from the stage, stating, "One of our greatest assets in this country are the talented boys and girls who devote their early lives to music, the appreciation of music, and an understanding of it." He went on to say that "emphasis upon artistic achievement in music is a source of satisfaction and pride to all of us."

GREATER BOSTON YOUTH SYMPHONY ORCHESTRA

MARVIN RABIN, *Conductor*

BRECKENRIDGE BOYS CHOIR
Breckenridge, Texas

MRS. BEN J. DEAN, JR., *Director*

Monday, April 16, 1962
South Lawn of the White House

The program for the White House concert included "Fanfare for the Common Man," the finale from Antonín Dvořák's *New World Symphony*, and the Berceuse and Finale from Igor Stravinsky's *Firebird Suite*. GBYSO also gave the premiere of *Tenso: Afternoon Music for Orchestra*, written specifically for the concert by Boston University alumnus Stanley Silverman.

Despite the cold weather and wind that threatened to blow music off stands, the orchestra impressed the audience of 700 guests with its performance. The president even remarked that he had "never heard the 'Star Spangled Banner' played with more enthusiasm and precision." Covered in national publications such as the *New York Times*, the concert gave the BYSO widespread recognition.

A letter from Jacqueline Kennedy, dated April 17, 1962, thanked conductor Dr. Marvin Rabin and GBYSO for the White House concert. The first lady wrote, "It was a most enjoyable afternoon, and there is no question but that the young boys and girls played beautifully . . . The President joins me in sending you all, along with our deep appreciation, our very best wishes."

THE WHITE HOUSE
WASHINGTON

April 17, 1962

Dear Mr. Rabin,

The President and I are indeed grateful to you, to the officers of the Greater Boston Youth Symphony, and to each and every member of the orchestra, for the wonderful concert you gave us yesterday. Certainly, it was a most enjoyable afternoon, and there is no question but that the young boys and girls played beautifully. We were very proud of them, and wish them great success in their musical careers.

I was very touched by the presents brought to me by the members of the symphony. Little John will love his Harvard sweater, and Caroline is delighted to have such a lovely Easter book about baby ducklings. It was most kind and thoughtful of the orchestra to bring these gifts.

I know how much work this has meant for all of you, particularly Dr. Max Kaplan, and The President joins me in sending you all, along with our deep appreciation, our very best wishes.

Sincerely,

Jacqueline Kennedy

Mr. Marvin Rabin
The Greater Boston Youth
    Symphony Orchestra
Boston University
855 Commonwealth Avenue
Boston, Massachusetts

Following their concert at the White House, the members of GBYSO spent the night at Fort Belvoir. The following day, the orchestra had the opportunity to tour Washington, D.C.; the young musicians visited the National Gallery of Art, Arlington Cemetery, and the United States Capitol before departing for New York.

After the successful performance at the White House, the orchestra traveled north to New York for a concert at Carnegie Hall. April 19, 1962, marked GBYSO's second appearance at the famed venue. Despite their final rehearsal being cut short by Leonard Bernstein rehearsing the New York Philharmonic overtime, the student musicians were thrilled with the performance.

24

Like GBYSO's debut at New England Conservatory's Jordan Hall in 1959, the concert at Carnegie Hall was named "A Salute to UNICEF." Cosponsored by *Seventeen* magazine and the United States Committee for UNICEF, the performance attracted many delegates from the United Nations. The program featured the pieces that had been presented at the White House. The concert was praised by *New York Times* critic Alan Rich, who wrote, "The orchestra, composed of 102 players from junior high and high schools in the Boston area, made some fine sounds. Its polish could shame many professional orchestras; its zest should shame them all. Mr. Rabin's skilled beat drew fine and poised sounds from his group, and showed considerable depth of insight."

In the fall of 1962, four years after the founding of the BYSO, 350 musicians auditioned for membership in the orchestra. In addition to full-orchestra rehearsals, the young musicians participated in sectionals each season. Above, trombonists (from left to right) David Schwartz (class of 1961), John Swan (class of 1962), and Erik Hoagland (class of 1963) rehearse at Boston University around 1961.

Greater
Boston
Youth
Symphony
Orchestra

JORDAN HALL
MAY 5, 1963 – 3 P.M.

MARVIN RABIN
Conductor

The 105 members of GBYSO in its fifth season had the opportunity to perform the finale of Ludwig van Beethoven's Symphony No. 9 with the Boston Symphony Orchestra in two young people's concerts under the direction of Harry Ellis Dickson. The annual concert at New England Conservatory's Jordan Hall featured soloist John Adams (class of 1964), now a renowned composer, performing Wolfgang Amadeus Mozart's Clarinet Concerto in A Major, as well as Nikolai Rimsky-Korsakov's *Capriccio Espagnol*.

A second orchestra, conducted by Dr. Artin Arslanian, was established in 1963 due to the demand created by the number of auditioning students. This group, originally called the Greater Boston Junior Youth Symphony Orchestra, made its debut on February 2, 1964, and is now known as the Repertory Orchestra. The more advanced orchestra retained the GBYSO name.

The Greater Boston
Junior
Youth Symphony Orchestra

ARTIN ARSLANIAN, *conductor*

in

FIRST ANNUAL CONCERT

Sunday, February 2, 1964   3.00 P. M.

CONCERT HALL

Boston University
School of Fine and Applied Arts
855 Commonwealth Avenue
Boston, Mass.

The sixth season began with the second summer workshop at Sargent Camp, which emphasized experience in chamber orchestra and chamber music ensembles. Composer and oboist Norman Leyden organized a conducting class, and many of his students had the opportunity to conduct the full orchestra during sight-reading sessions.

In August 1963, 110 GBYSO students attended the workshop at Sargent Camp in Peterborough, New Hampshire, including alternates and some members of the Greater Boston Junior Youth Symphony Orchestra. The group was invited by the Peterborough City Council to present an outdoor evening concert, which featured works by Richard Wagner and Carl Maria von Weber. Above, Dr. Marvin Rabin conducts the full orchestra outdoors in a rehearsal during the workshop.

Here the double basses participate in an outdoor sectional rehearsal during the 1963 summer workshop. Both the faculty and the students presented chamber music concerts while at Sargent Camp, and violinist Roman Totenberg conducted a master class for string players. The week ended on August 30 with an open rehearsal for parents and friends that included Symphony No. 2 by Johannes Brahms.

The sixth season included GBYSO's first concert at Boston's acclaimed Symphony Hall on February 23, 1964. With the Greater Boston Junior Youth Symphony Orchestra also on the concert bill, the two orchestras performed a long program, including Jean Sibelius's *Finlandia*, the finale of Johannes Brahms's Symphony No. 1, Johann Sebastian Bach's Brandenburg Concerto No. 4 in G Major, and works by Dmitri Kabalevsky, George Enesco, and others.

Concerts for Young People

LITTLE THEATER

Lowell State College

1963 - 1964

During the 1963–1964 season, GBYSO presented a concert at Lowell State College sponsored by a local group called Concerts for Young People. The performance included works by Johann Strauss and Brahms, as well as Maurice Ravel's Introduction and Allegro, which highlighted talented soloists from the orchestra.

In 1964, GBYSO was featured in 13 biweekly radio broadcasts, each an hour long, sponsored by the Boston Gas Company. The company paid the orchestra $125 per broadcast, and the series included music from recordings and tapes made over five years, as well as interviews and performances from the summer workshop.

At the beginning of the 1964–1965 season, Dr. Artin Arslanian became the second music director of the BYSO. Arslanian, who had conducted the Greater Boston Junior Youth Symphony Orchestra, continued Dr. Marvin Rabin's commitment to artistic excellence, leading GBYSO in performances at New England Conservatory's Jordan Hall and Boston's Symphony Hall until 1967.

In 1967, Dr. Walter Eisenberg was appointed the third music director of the BYSO. An associate professor of music at Boston University, Eisenberg served the organization for 13 years, until 1980. Under his leadership, GBYSO traveled in 1969 to Switzerland on the first of many international tours.

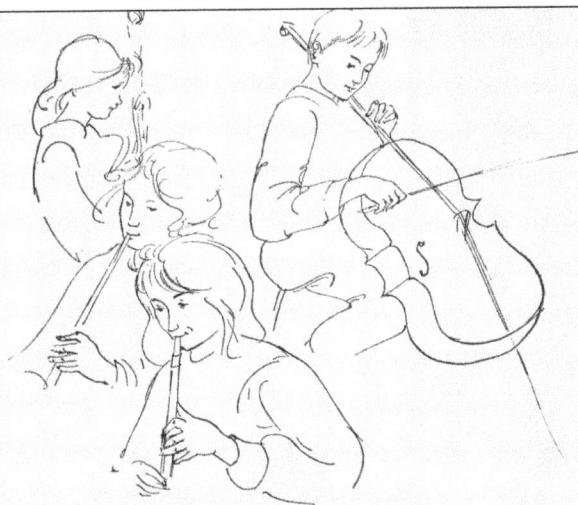

THE GREATER BOSTON
YOUTH SYMPHONY ORCHESTRA

1958-1968

Symphony Hall   April 21, 1968

Led by Eisenberg, the orchestra performed its 10th anniversary concert at Boston's Symphony Hall on April 21, 1968. The program, which included 20th-century works by Paul Hindemith and Ottorino Respighi, was accompanied by a message from the conductor, stating "It is an important challenge for young players today to be able to present a program of their own time."

31

From left to right, Geoffrey Hall (class of 1971), Dean Witten (class of 1969), Richard Kravetz (class of 1970), and Ken O'Toole (class of 1969), all members of GBYSO's percussion section, rehearse at Boston University in August 1969 in preparation for their performances scheduled to take place later that month while on tour in Switzerland.

A free send-off concert was held at Boston's City Hall Plaza on August 15, 1969, where the orchestra performed some of the music that it later presented on tour in St. Moritz, Zurich, and Geneva.

The program at City Hall Plaza included Paul Hindemith's *Symphonic Metamorphoses* and Max Bruch's Concerto for Violin in G minor with soloist Ronan Lefkowitz (class of 1970), who would later become a member of the Boston Symphony Orchestra.

Boston City Hall Concert

AUGUST 15, 1969

12:00 Noon

The International Festival of Youth Orchestras

St. Moritz, August 18-30, 1969

The musicians departed for the BYSO's first international tour on August 18, 1969. In St. Moritz, the orchestra earned top honors at the first International Festival of Youth Orchestras. The festival, which took place from August 18 until August 30, featured young musicians from England, Canada, Norway, Holland, Finland, the Czech Republic, Poland, Switzerland, and other areas of the United States. Twenty BYSO students were selected to play in the final concert under the baton of conductor Leopold Stokowski.

The Commonwealth of Massachusetts

Francis W. Sargent
Governor

to

Greater Boston Youth Symphony Orchestra
for its overwhelming success as outstanding orchestra
at the International Festival of Youth Orchestras
in St. Moritz, Switzerland
which is deserving of recognition by all the citizens of Massachusetts.

Witness my hand and the Seal of the Commonwealth of Massachusetts, this twenty-third day of September in the year of Our Lord 1969

Witness the Great Seal of the Commonwealth

On September 23, 1969, after GBYSO's return from Switzerland, Massachusetts governor Francis W. Sargent issued a commendation praising the orchestra for "its overwhelming success as outstanding orchestra at the International Festival of Youth Orchestras in St. Moritz, Switzerland, which is deserving of recognition by all the citizens of Massachusetts."

Gov. Francis W. Sargent signs the commendation in his office at the statehouse with Dr. Walter Eisenberg (far left) and members of GBYSO in attendance.

Two

FROM 1970 TO 1979

During the 1970s, the BYSO celebrated its 20th anniversary season, marking two decades of commitment to nurturing young people in the tradition of classical music. Dr. Walter Eisenberg remained the music director of the organization until 1980, leading tours to Israel, Great Britain, Colombia, and West Germany and Belgium. Other highlights of the decade included a performance at the Kennedy Center in Washington, D.C., a televised collaboration with the Boston Ballet, concerts at the Hatch Memorial Shell on the Charles River Esplanade, and annual summer workshops held at Agassiz Village in Maine.

On March 8, 1970, GBYSO presented a concert of 20th-century music at Harvard University's Sanders Theatre in celebration of Boston University's centennial year. The program featured Roman Totenberg performing Krzysztof Penderecki's Capriccio for Violin and Orchestra, Dmitri Shostakovich's Symphony No. 5, and the United States premiere of Michal Spisak's *Symphonie Concertante*.

In the summer of 1970, GBYSO made history as the first foreign youth orchestra to perform at the prestigious Israel Festival of Music and Drama. The young musicians departed on August 10, 1970, and spent more than two weeks in Israel before returning to Boston.

As rehearsals began for the 1970 tour to Israel, some people expressed concern about the country's uncertain climate. In a letter to BYSO president Dr. Phyllis Kuffler, Dean Edwin E. Stein wrote, "There is perhaps in many of us an element of apprehension about the responsibility for sending a group of students to this country as we hear and read reports of violence and other unsettled conditions." Stein acknowledged that all possible precautions should be taken but firmly stated at the end of his letter, "I am for the trip." The BYSO presented a tour benefit concert at Symphony Hall on April 19, 1970. Both of the organization's orchestras performed, and the concert was broadcast live on the radio. The program stated, "GBYSO's participation in the Israel Festival of Music and Drama is a clear statement of the belief that our youth can represent this country and its music at the highest possible level, it is an investment in international understanding, in world harmony."

THE TENTH ISRAEL FESTIVAL 1970

While in Israel, the orchestra performed alongside renowned musicians from all over the world. The festival opened with Zubin Mehta conducting the Israel Philharmonic Orchestra; other acclaimed performers in attendance included Isaac Stern, Daniel Barenboim, Leonard Rose, Maureen Forrester, Pablo Casals, and the Juilliard String Quartet.

The orchestra performed works by Mikhail Glinka, Paul Hindemith, Krzysztof Penderecki, Leonard Bernstein, Garner Read, and Zoltán Kodály at concerts in Caesarea, Jerusalem, Tel Aviv, and Nof Ginosar. In a book of impressions compiled by the BYSO following the tour, one student wrote that the Roman amphitheater in Caesarea was "so close to the Mediterranean that I walked out and watched the waves under a full moon at intermission."

In addition to rehearsals and concerts, the orchestra participated in sightseeing excursions throughout the trip to Israel; GBYSO members had the opportunity to visit Jaffa, Nazareth, the Dome of the Rock, the Israel Museum, the Dead Sea, the Judean desert, the Sea of Galilee, Bethlehem, and the John F. Kennedy Peace Forest.

> the best proof of their great succes was the fact that the audience did not leave the auditorium at the end of the program and called for "encore".
>
> Your admirable Youth Orchestra with their conductor Walter Eisenberg, a musician of great culture and sensibility, one of those who are advancing the art of music, and with the excellent soloist Roman Totenberg, have represented their country splendidly with devotion and love to music. You can be proud of the high artistic level achieved by your Youth Orchestra.
>
> With my best wishes and hope to hear them again.
>
> Yours sincerely,   Dan Aronowicz

Following the tour, the BYSO received a handwritten letter from Dan Aronowicz, a music critic for a newspaper called *L'Information d'Israel*. Of the young musicians, he wrote, "The best proof of their great success was the fact that the audience did not leave the auditorium at the end of the program and called for an encore."

The BYSO continued to hold summer workshops throughout the 1970s. At Agassiz Village in Poland, Maine, members of the orchestras devoted a week each summer to intensive study of orchestral and chamber music repertoire in an informal camp setting. The workshop also allowed the young musicians to get to know one another before the start of each season.

Violinists (from left to right) Mary Connors (class of 1973) and Linda Nichols (class of 1973) add markings to their music at a GBYSO rehearsal during the 1971–1972 season. The repertoire that year included works by Antonín Dvořák, Nikolai Rimsky-Korsakov, Witold Lutoslawski, and Gustav Mahler, as well as an overture written by Robert Beaser, the winner of a composition competition sponsored by GBYSO.

The 1971–1972 season included a performance at Phillips Academy in Andover as well as a pops concert presented by the Greater Boston Junior Youth Symphony Orchestra under the direction of Robert Corley. Here musicians (from left to right) Roberta Benotti (class of 1972), Scott Drew (class of 1973), Ellen Donohue (class of 1973), and Michael Strauss (class of 1972) pose with their instruments at Boston University's College of Fine Arts.

Members of GBYSO's brass section rehearse with a coach at Boston University's College of Fine Arts during the 1971–1972 season. On March 5, 1972, GBYSO performed at the Roberts Center at Boston College. The concert program included Dvořák's *Carnival Overture* and movements from Mahler's Symphony No. 1 and Rimsky-Korsakov's *Scheherazade*.

You are cordially invited as guest of

Mrs. Edward Kennedy
Honorary Concert Chairman

and the

Board of Directors of GBYSO

to attend a Concert by

The Greater Boston Youth Symphony Orchestra
Walter Eisenberg, Conductor

Sunday afternoon, May 21, 1972 at 3 o'clock

Kennedy Center for the Performing Arts

Admit Two — If you are unable to attend, please extend this invitation to
friends who share your interest in Youth and Fine Music.

In 1972, GBYSO returned to Washington, D.C., this time to perform at the Kennedy Center. Sponsored by American Airlines in cooperation with the American Youth Performs Foundation, the concert on May 21, 1972, featured Antonín Dvořák's *Carnival Overture*, Nikolai Rimsky-Korsakov's *Scheherazade*, and Witold Lutoslawski's Concerto for Orchestra.

```
THURSDAY  JUNE 29           LONDON
FULL BREAKFAST served aloft.

Land Heathrow Airport.   11:10 A.M.

Disembark and proceed through the
British immigration into the
customs hall.

Here you will be met by your
couriers and representatives of
ACFEA who will escort you to the
motorcoaches and arrange collection
of your luggage.

TRANSFER to HOTEL GROSVENOR VICTORIA
                     (2 Nights)

Late LUNCH in the hotel immediately
followed by a BRIEFING on the
arrangements for the next 18 days.

In the late afternoon rest and get
unpacked.
```

In July 1972, GBYSO toured England, Scotland, and Wales. During the trip, the orchestra presented concerts at Guildford Civic Hall, Eton College Chapel, Brangwyn Hall in Swansea, Whitehaven Civic Hall, and George Watson's College in Edinburgh. The orchestra performed many of the pieces that it had played at the Kennedy Center, with the addition of Gustav Mahler's Symphony No. 1. The pocket-size itinerary carried by each musician explained the details of the trip.

The orchestra departed on June 28, 1972, for an 18-day tour of Great Britain. In London, the young musicians had the opportunity to visit Westminster Abbey, Big Ben, and other landmarks. Above, musicians (from left to right) Neal Kravitz (class of 1975), Pamela Griffen (class of 1972), James Orent (class of 1972), and Glen Walant (class of 1972) stand with a guard outside the gates of Buckingham Palace.

After a day of sightseeing, the musicians began to prepare for the first concert at Guildford Civic Hall. Trombonist Dana Cohen (class of 1972) sits beside his exhausted friend Tom Williams (class of 1974) at a rehearsal in London.

After an excursion to Stonehenge, the orchestra presented a concert at Eton College Chapel, which was taped by the BBC and later broadcast as part of a series on youth and music. From London, the group traveled to Wales. On July 7, 1972, the orchestra performed at Brangwyn Hall in Swansea (shown here).

On December 13, 1972, the Jordan Marsh Company in conjunction with WNAC Television presented a holiday concert featuring GBYSO and the Boston Ballet. Choreographer Samuel Kurkjian collaborated with Dr. Walter Eisenberg in planning the performance.

At the December 13, 1972, holiday concert, bright lights illuminate the stage from every angle as GBYSO performs *Roman Carnival Overture* by Hector Berlioz, Samuel Barber's *Die Natali*, the third movement of Franz Joseph Haydn's Trumpet Concerto, and Alexander Borodin's "Polovtsian Dances" from the opera *Prince Igor*. Led by Dr. Walter Eisenberg, the orchestra was surrounded by a backdrop of curtains and statuesque cutouts that decorated the studio; the ensemble even had its own sparkling GBYSO sign. Dancers from the Boston Ballet joined the orchestra to present selections from *The Nutcracker Suite* by Pyotr Ilich Tchaikovsky, and the concert ended with Maurice Ravel's *Boléro*.

In June 1974, GBYSO traveled to Colombia for a 10-day tour. While in South America the orchestra presented four concerts in Bogota and Medellin, performing Pyotr Ilich Tchaikovsky's Symphony No. 5, the Prelude to Richard Wagner's *Die Meistersinger von Nürnberg*, George Gershwin's *An American in Paris*, Antonio Vivaldi's Concerto for Four Violins, selected movements from Hector Berlioz's *Symphonie Fantastique*, waltzes from Richard Strauss's opera *Der Rosenkavalier*, and other works by Manuel de Falla and Frederick Delius. GBYSO was also featured on Colombian national television. During the tour, Dr. Walter Eisenberg and members of the orchestra met with local educators to help promote the creation of music programs for high school students. The orchestra performed at the Basilica Metropolitana in Medellin on June 24 and 25, 1974. The venue (shown here) was packed with listeners.

During the Colombia tour, the orchestra's activities and concerts in Medellin, Boston's sister city, were planned by Partners of the Americas, an independent organization that arranged cultural, economic, social, and other exchanges between the United States and Central America. Fabricato, one of Colombia's largest textile companies, also helped plan the events of the tour.

JUNIO 24 BASILICA METROPOLITANA.
25 BASILICA METROPOLITANA.
26 TEATRO PABLO TOBON URIBE.*

LOS AMIGOS DE LAS AMERICAS
(MASSACHUSETTS - ANTIOQUIA)
Y LA UNIVERSIDAD DE BOSTON
SE COMPLACEN EN PRESENTAR LA

ORQUESTA SINFONICA JUVENIL DE BOSTON

DIRECTOR: WALTER EISENBERG.

PATROCINA :

Fabricato

* A beneficio de la CLINICA NOEL.

The Board of Directors in
Association with Boston University
proudly presents
The Greater Boston Youth Symphony Orchestras
In Concert
Walter Eisenberg, conductor-music director

March 9, 1975   Symphony Hall   3:00 P. M.

On March 9, 1975, GBYSO gave a concert at Symphony Hall in which the string sections of the two full orchestras combined to perform "Fantasia on a Theme by Thomas Tallis" by Ralph Vaughan Williams. The program also included movements from Sergei Prokofiev's *Lieutenant Kije Suite*, Igor Stravinsky's *Petrouchka*, and Maurice Ravel's *La Valse*.

47

Pictured here conducting a rehearsal during the 1974–1975 season, Dr. Walter Eisenberg wrote in the March 9, 1975, concert program, "Each year at this time, as I evaluate our GBYSO program, there is a great sense of pride and satisfaction in witnessing the remarkable development of our student musicians. As we work on the plans for next season I find my enthusiasm greater than ever for what we will be able to do for our students."

Sectional rehearsals have been an important part of the BYSO since the organization's foundation. In these rehearsals, each section of the orchestra works with a specialized coach. Members of the horn section practice their orchestra parts with an instructor at Boston University's College of Fine Arts during the 1975–1976 season.

The repertoire for the 1975–1976 season included challenging pieces such as Maurice Ravel's arrangement of Modest Petrovich Mussorgsky's *Pictures at an Exhibition*, Antonio Vivaldi's Concerto for Four Violins, and George Gershwin's *Rhapsody in Blue*. Here musicians (from left to right) Adam Gonzalez (class of 1977), Elliott Markow (class of 1977), David Dubiel (class of 1977), and Melanie Macaronis (class of 1978) pose together in black and white concert dress at a GBYSO performance that season.

In the fall of 1976, Sir Colin Davis, principal guest conductor of the Boston Symphony Orchestra from 1972 to 1984, led a GBYSO rehearsal at Boston University's College of Fine Arts. Conductor Michael Tilson Thomas also visited GBYSO that season.

Boston University
and
GBYSO Board of Directors
Proudly Present

The Greater Boston
Youth Symphony Orchestras
Walter Eisenberg, Conductor
in its
Gala 20th Anniversary Concert

Symphony Hall, Boston
April 9, 1978

During the 1977–1978 season, the BYSO celebrated its 20th anniversary. On April 9, 1978, the organization presented a gala concert at Symphony Hall to mark the occasion. The orchestras performed Samuel Barber's Adagio for Strings and Ludwig van Beethoven's *Choral Fantasy in C Minor*, as well as works by Giovanni Gabrieli, Camille Saint-Saëns, and Nikolai Rimsky-Korsakov. In the concert program, Dr. Walter Eisenberg wrote, "For 20 years, GBYSO has served youth and music. It has influenced the lives and directions of students who have not only gone into successful musical careers, but many of whom are achieving recognition and distinction in numerous fields other than music . . . It is significant that regardless of the careers they have pursued, the majority of GBYSO alumni still keep up with music in some form."

In October and November 1978, members of GBYSO shared music stands with Boston Symphony Orchestra musicians in five youth concert performances of Pyotr Ilich Tchaikovsky's *1812 Overture* under the direction of Harry Ellis Dickson. The concerts took place at Boston's Symphony Hall.

On December 17, 1978, both of the BYSO's orchestras performed at the Church of the Immaculate Conception in Boston. The holiday concert included the finale of Jean Sibelius's Symphony No. 2, George Gershwin's *An American in Paris*, and other works by Guiseppe Verdi, Dmitri Kabalevsky, and Nikolai Rimsky-Korsakov.

Nicholas Macaronis, then president of the BYSO's board of directors, wrote in the December 17, 1978, holiday concert program that through "hard work, self-discipline, and commitment to a high standard" the BYSO's young musicians gained "an invaluable experience not only as orchestra members but as individuals, wherever their career paths take them."

On March 18, 1979, GBYSO presented a concert at New England Conservatory's Jordan Hall featuring works by Dmitri Kabalevsky, Franz Joseph Haydn, Franz Liszt, Igor Stravinsky, and George Gershwin. During the concert, GBYSO announced that it had accepted an invitation to perform in South America later that year. Rehearsals during the remainder of the season were dedicated to preparing for the tour.

In 1979, GBYSO returned to Colombia by popular demand for a 10-day tour. The orchestra presented a farewell concert on the Charles River Esplanade at the Hatch Memorial Shell on June 13, 1979, that featured many of the pieces that would be performed during the trip, including works by Alexander Borodin, George Gershwin, and Pyotr Ilich Tchaikovsky.

The orchestra departed for South America on June 15, 1979. Sponsored by Partners of the Americas in celebration of the United Nations International Year of the Child, the tour included six performances in Bogota, Tunja, Medellin, and Rio Negro, as well as appearances on national television and radio.

In Colombia, the orchestra performed at multiple venues, including Theatre Colon, Theatre Pablo Tobon Uribe, the Cathedral of Rio Negro, and Basilica Metropolitana in Medellin. GBYSO also presented a special benefit concert in Medellin for the Clinica Noel, the children's hospital of the province of Antioquia. Pictured here is the orchestra's performance at the Cathedral of Rio Negro on June 19, 1979.

The repertoire performed in South America included Carl Maria von Weber's Overture to *Oberon*, Franz Joseph Haydn's Trumpet Concerto, Franz Liszt's *Les Préludes*, Igor Stravinsky's *Firebird Suite*, George Gershwin's *An American in Paris*, Alexander Borodin's "Polovtsian Dances" from the opera *Prince Igor*, and Pyotr Ilich Tchaikovsky's *1812 Overture*. Dr. Walter Eisenberg conducted the orchestra at the Basilica Metropolitana in Medellin (shown here) on June 20, 1979.

Large, enthusiastic audiences were a constant throughout the tour. After concerts, listeners often lingered to talk to the orchestra members and help pack instruments.

With the beautiful decorations of the hall sparkling in the background, curious children crowd around the stage to get a glimpse of the musicians and their instruments before GYBSO's performance at Theatre Colon.

The 1979–1980 season included plans for an exchange with the Düsseldorf Youth Symphony Orchestra as well as a benefit concert for the Kennedy Memorial Hospital for Children. Preparations for the season and a new decade of music began at the annual summer workshop at Agassiz Village in Maine, where Dr. Walter Eisenberg and GBYSO's coaching staff led a week of sectionals, chamber music rehearsals, and full-orchestra rehearsals.

Three

FROM 1980 TO 1989

Dr. Walter Eisenberg conducted his final GBYSO concerts during a tour to West Germany and Belgium in 1980. GBYSO members continued to participate in international tours throughout the next decade, including trips to Montreal, Paris, central Europe, and Japan. The BYSO became an independent nonprofit organization in 1983, marking a significant change in the daily operations of the program. Music directors Leonard Atherton and Eiji Oue led the orchestra members at summer workshops and in concerts at major venues in the Boston area, and by the BYSO's 30th anniversary season in 1988, the organization had grown to include 200 members in two full orchestras, a chamber orchestra, and percussion, brass, and wind ensembles.

GBYSO participated in an exchange with young musicians from Germany in March 1980. The Düsseldorf Youth Symphony Orchestra traveled to Massachusetts to perform in the Boston area and meet with GBYSO students. Members of the orchestra stayed with GBYSO families and presented a concert featuring works by Wolfgang Amadeus Mozart, Franz Joseph Haydn, and Johannes Brahms at Harvard University's Sanders Theatre.

GBYSO completed the exchange with the Düsseldorf Youth Symphony Orchestra by traveling to Düsseldorf in the spring of 1980 to perform as part of a tour to West Germany and Belgium. The musicians departed on April 19, 1980, and stayed with German host families while in Düsseldorf.

The programs in West Germany and Belgium included *Roman Carnival Overture* by Hector Berlioz and *Variations on "America"* by Charles Ives, as well as Nikolai Rimsky-Korsakov's *Scheherazade* and Paul Hindemith's *Symphonic Metamorphoses*. After 13 years of leadership, Dr. Walter Eisenberg conducted his final GBYSO performances during this tour.

Leonard Atherton became the BYSO's fourth music director in 1980. In the winter 1981 GBYSO newsletter, he wrote, "I look forward to a season of rewards . . . the Jordan Hall concert program, coming up on May 8, is one of the most challenging that GBYSO has undertaken, and I trust in the talent, ability, and commitment of each player to rise to that challenge."

During the 1980–1981 season, GBYSO performed a variety of pieces, including Gioachino Rossini's Overture to *Semiramide*, Max Bruch's Concerto for Violin in G minor, Georges Bizet's Suite No. 1 from *Carmen*, and Leonard Bernstein's Symphonic Dances from *West Side Story*. The holiday concert at Boston's Church of the Immaculate Conception on December 7, 1980, featured the Boston Public Schools All-City Chorus singing Robert Winfrey's "Let's Build a City" and Earl Robinson's "Ballad for Americans." On April 5, 1981, GBYSO's gala concert at Symphony Hall (shown here) featured the combined choruses of the Commonwealth School, Concord Academy, and Quabbin, Stoneham, and Wachusett High Schools performing *Dona nobis pacem* by Ralph Vaughan Williams. The program also included works by Emmanuel Chabrier, Aaron Copland, and Aram Khachaturian; the concert ended with Leonard Atherton conducting Dmitri Shostakovich's Symphony No. 5.

Leonard Atherton's tenure as music director included a tour to Montreal in 1982 during which GBYSO performed in local schools and with the Montreal Youth Orchestra in a joint public concert. Here GBYSO principal cellist Leslie Wu (class of 1983) plays in a rehearsal alongside members of the Westmount High School band.

In 1982, Eiji Oue became the youngest music director of the BYSO at age 25. Born in Hiroshima, Japan, Oue studied at the Toho School of Music in Tokyo and then at the New England Conservatory of Music. During the 1982–1983 season, the organization's highest-level orchestra, conducted by Oue, became informally known as the Senior Orchestra.

Eiji Oue's early appearances with GBYSO included concerts at New England Conservatory's Jordan Hall and Boston's Symphony Hall, where he conducted pieces such as Igor Stravinsky's *Firebird Suite*, Wolfgang Amadeus Mozart's Symphony No. 40, and Pyotr Ilich Tchaikovsky's *The Nutcracker Suite*. In the April 17, 1983, concert program, he wrote, "On the first day that I conducted a GBYSO rehearsal as its Music Director, I discovered so many talented students here who loved music that I felt overwhelmed with the responsibility of guiding them through the repertoire. This, I believed, would be a monumental task. Since that day, the orchestra has always responded very well and we have developed a working partnership which you will hear today . . . during this anniversary year, we have become a family." In 1983, just a few months after Oue's arrival, the BYSO became an independent nonprofit organization.

As part of the BYSO's 25th anniversary season, the organization commissioned a piece by Boston University composer Theodore Antoniou, whose work, *The GBYSO Music*, was premiered on April 17, 1983, at Symphony Hall. In the same concert, the Senior Orchestra performed Ludwig van Beethoven's Symphony No. 9 with Masterworks Chorale.

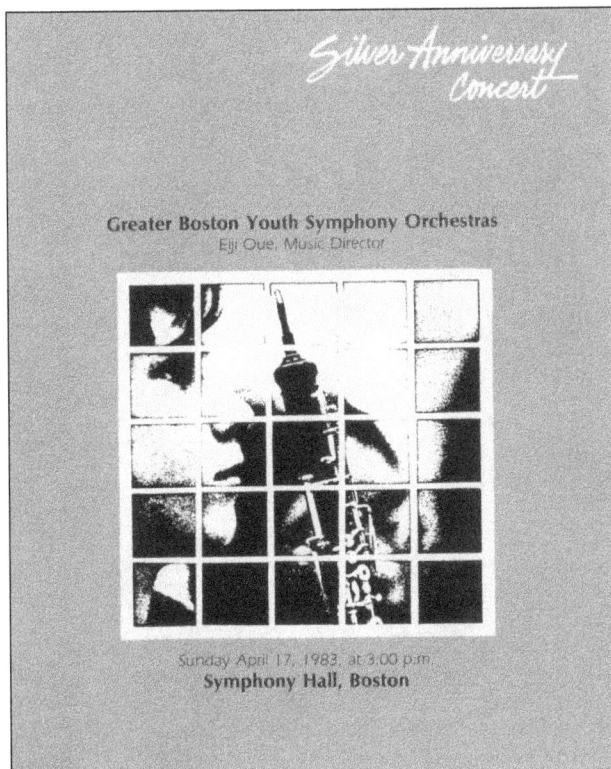

Silver Anniversary Concert

Greater Boston Youth Symphony Orchestras
Eji Oue, Music Director

Sunday April 17, 1983, at 3:00 p.m.
Symphony Hall, Boston

The Senior Orchestra traveled to France in June 1983 at the invitation of the French Ministry of Culture. The orchestra presented concerts in multiple cities during the tour. Huge stone columns, pointed arches, and stained glass surrounded the orchestra at a performance at Saint-Leu d'Esserent (shown here).

At Saint-Leu d'Esserent, the orchestra gave a concert for 500 children. Following the performance, the eager listeners crowded around members of the orchestra and even asked for autographs. Outside the abbey, young fans surround tuba player John Manning (class of 1983).

During the tour of France, the orchestra performed at many venues, including Saint-Leu d'Esserent, Chateau de Malmaison, Église Saint-Louis des Invalides, and an outdoor stage constructed for La Fête de la Musique. Eiji Oue also conducted the Senior Orchestra at Cathedral Saint-Étienne de Meaux (pictured here).

The orchestra presented six concerts while on tour in France. In addition to these performances, the young musicians had the opportunity to sightsee in Paris. They visited cathedrals and museums and even spent a day in the French countryside; riding in buses quickly became routine.

Members of the Senior Orchestra performed at the national Fête de la Musique on an outdoor stage built specifically for the event at the foot of Montmartre. The free concert, which was broadcast live over Radio Luxembourg, drew approximately 10,000 spectators. The performance also featured vocalists Nana Mouskouri and Guy Béart.

Members of the brass section perform on the outdoor stage as part of the orchestra's performance at Lae Fête de la Musique. During the 10-day trip to Paris, Eiji Oue led the orchestra in works by Richard Wagner, Igor Stravinsky, Maurice Ravel, Gustav Holst, Pyotr Ilich Tchaikovsky, and Gioachino Rossini. The tour marked the final event of GBYSO's 25th anniversary season.

In 1983, Leonard Bernstein conducted GBYSO at his 65th birthday concert in Lawrence, Massachusetts. The 1983–1984 season included performances at Harvard University's Sanders Theatre, the Isabella Stewart Gardner Museum, and Symphony Hall. Pictured above is a GBYSO performance at the Hatch Memorial Shell on the Charles River Esplanade in Boston during the summer of 1984.

In 1985, the Senior Orchestra embarked on a two-week tour of Yugoslavia, Hungary, and Austria. The tour send-off concert on June 9, 1985, included Igor Stravinsky's *The Rite of Spring* and other works by Aaron Copland, Johannes Brahms, and Béla Bartók. The trip featured a performance in Budapest for an audience of 1,200 at the Fifth International Congress of International Physicians for the Prevention of Nuclear War, as well as an appearance at the Dubrovnik Music Festival.

GREATER BOSTON YOUTH
SYMPHONY ORCHESTRAS

EIJI OUE, Music Director
27th Season, 1984-1985

TOUR SEND-OFF CONCERT

SENIOR ORCHESTRA
Sunday, June 9, 1985
3:00 P.M.
Sanders Theatre

GBYSO is sponsored by Boston University

and a community board of directors

Eiji Oue led GBYSO in many challenging pieces during the 1985–1986 season. The GBYSO Chamber Orchestra performed Ludwig van Beethoven's Overture to *Fidelio*, Johann Sebastian Bach's Brandenburg Concerto No. 2, and Beethoven's Symphony No. 8. On April 30, 1986, the Senior Orchestra presented Gustav Mahler's Symphony No. 5 at Boston's Symphony Hall.

The BYSO continued to hold annual summer workshops throughout the 1980s. Each season started off at Agassiz Village in Maine with intensive coaching in chamber music, sectionals, and full-orchestra rehearsals. New and returning members of the orchestras had the opportunity to get to know one another at camp and work on repertoire for the upcoming year.

Members of GBYSO's violin section rehearse prior to a concert in 1987. That year, Mayor Raymond Flynn proclaimed April 12 Greater Boston Youth Symphony Orchestra Day in honor of the organization's outstanding service to young musicians and the people of Boston. On Greater Boston Youth Symphony Orchestra Day, the Senior and Repertory Orchestras performed works by Antonín Dvořák, Ferdinand David, and Johannes Brahms at New England Conservatory's Jordan Hall.

During the 1987–1988 season, the Repertory Orchestra performed multiple works, including Richard Wagner's Overture to *Die Meistersinger von Nürnberg* and Franz Schubert's Symphony No. 8 ("The Unfinished"). The Senior Orchestra presented Richard Strauss's *Don Juan* and Gustav Mahler's Symphony No. 1 at New England Conservatory's Jordan Hall on December 6, 1987. Here Michael Graham (class of 1988) plays cello during a GBYSO rehearsal.

On March 6, 1988, GBYSO musicians joined members of the Boston Symphony Orchestra and the New England Conservatory Youth Philharmonic Orchestra at the opening of the Hynes Convention Center in Boston's Back Bay. John Williams conducted Dvořák's Concerto for Cello with soloist Yo-Yo Ma, and Harry Ellis Dickson conducted the third movement of Pyotr Ilich Tchaikovsky's Symphony No. 6. Here GBYSO performs at Jordan Hall around 1988.

The BYSO's 30th anniversary gala concert on April 10, 1988, at Symphony Hall featured the Senior Orchestra performing Gustav Mahler's Symphony No. 2 ("Resurrection") with contralto Maureen Forrester, soprano Luvenia Garner, and the combined Concord Chorus and Newton Choral Society. In the concert program, conductor Eiji Oue wrote, "Every time I see the Repertory Orchestra, you impress me with your tremendous musical growth. For the Senior Orchestra, I have set the highest standards; you continue to surprise me by not only reaching but exceeding those goals . . . In one week, GBYSO will be going to my country. My family and friends will hear one of the best youth orchestras in the world, and I am very proud to be taking them on this tour."

In 1988, the Senior Orchestra embarked on a tour of Japan, marking the BYSO's first trip to Asia. One hundred and twenty orchestra members, staff, chaperones, and members of the board of directors departed on April 15, 1988, and spent a week performing, traveling, and experiencing Japanese culture. Leonard Bernstein and Seiji Ozawa served as the tour's honorary chairs. The orchestra presented concerts in Tokyo, Hiroshima, Kyoto, and Osaka; the first performance at Hitomi Memorial Hall in Tokyo featured *Don Juan* by Richard Strauss, Niccolò Paganini's Violin Concerto No. 1 with concerto competition winner Vali Phillips, and Gustav Mahler's Symphony No. 1. After traveling by bullet train to Hiroshima, the birthplace of Eiji Oue, the orchestra performed Mahler's Symphony No. 2 ("Resurrection") in Yubinchokin Hall. Here the orchestra rehearses at Sun Plaza in Hiroshima.

At Sun Plaza in Hiroshima (shown here), the orchestra performed for 5,000 children. The program included Leonard Bernstein's Overture to *Candide*, movements of Pyotr Ilich Tchaikovsky's Symphony No. 6 ("Pathétique"), movements of Gustav Mahler's Symphony No. 1 and Symphony No. 2, and John Philip Sousa's "Stars and Stripes Forever." In Kyoto, Boston's sister city, the orchestra performed with the Horikawa High School Orchestra, and members of the Senior Orchestra stayed with Japanese hosts. In addition to performing, the young musicians visited many Japanese landmarks, including Miajima Island Shrine, Hiroshima's Peace Park, Kyoto's temples, and the Ginza in Tokyo.

WORLD PREMIERE

Sunday, June 12, 1988
7 p.m.
Sanders Theatre

To celebrate the BYSO's 30th anniversary in 1988, the BYSO commissioned noted composer Peter Lieberson to write a piece for "alumni and orchestra." The work, titled *The Gesar Legend*, featured five BYSO graduates who had joined the Boston Symphony Orchestra: Lawrence Wolfe (class of 1966), Fenwick Smith (class of 1967), Ronan Lefkowitz (class of 1970), Richard Sebring (class of 1974), and Sato Knudsen (class of 1975). *The Gesar Legend*, which draws on accounts of a heroic Tibetan warrior king, was premiered by the Senior Orchestra on June 12, 1988, at Harvard University's Sanders Theatre. Richard Dyer of the *Boston Globe* wrote in an article dated June 14, 1988, "Lieberson has been fortunate in the performers who have advanced his music, but many other composers might envy the caliber of the first performance that conductor Eiji Oue and GBYSO gave to *The Gesar Legend*—not to mention the attentiveness and enthusiasm of its audience."

After seven seasons as the music director of the BYSO, Eiji Oue conducted his last concert on December 16, 1988, at New England Conservatory's Jordan Hall. The performance featured internationally acclaimed pianist Peter Serkin playing Maurice Ravel's Piano Concerto in G Major with the Senior Orchestra. Here Oue and Serkin confer onstage after a rehearsal of the concerto.

Eiji Oue's last rehearsal with the Senior Orchestra took place onstage at New England Conservatory's Jordan Hall. In addition to Ravel's Piano Concerto in G Major, Oue's final concert included the Senior Orchestra performing Symphony No. 4 by Johannes Brahms; the Repertory Orchestra also presented Suite No. 1 from *Carmen* by Georges Bizet.

David Commanday became the sixth music director of the BYSO at the beginning of the 1989–1990 season. In a 1989 interview he stated, "GBYSO has an exciting future before it . . . I am looking forward to working with the students, to making music together, to traveling around the world on tour, and to making recordings."

David Commanday conducted the GBYSO Chamber Orchestra in works by Giovanni Gabrieli, Wolfgang Amadeus Mozart, Anton Webern, Claude Debussy, Carlos Chávez, and Pyotr Ilich Tchaikovsky at Boston University's Tsai Performance Center on November 11, 1989. His debut concert conducting the full Senior Orchestra took place at New England Conservatory's Jordan Hall on December 3, 1989; the combined Senior and Repertory Orchestras (pictured above) filled the stage for part of the concert.

The December 3, 1989, concert at New England Conservatory's Jordan Hall began with alumnus Joel Bard (class of 1980), the newly appointed conductor of the Repertory Orchestra, leading Four Dances from *Rodeo* by Aaron Copland. The Senior and Repertory Orchestras then joined forces to perform Antonín Dvořák's *Carnival Overture*; over 130 musicians were onstage, and each member of the Senior Orchestra sat next to a member of the Repertory Orchestra. The sold-out concert ended with David Commanday leading the Senior Orchestra in a performance of Sergei Rachmaninoff's Symphony No. 2. Alan Tommasini of the *Boston Globe* wrote in his review of the concert, "This was a carnival of a performance with go-for-broke enthusiasm and more full-bodied orchestral sound than I've heard anywhere in years." It seems fitting that this concert, marked by new leadership, launched the BYSO into a new decade of music making.

Four

FROM 1990 TO 1999

As the music director of the BYSO for most of the 1990s, David Commanday led the Senior Orchestra on tours of central Europe, Scandinavia, Italy, and England and Ireland. The Senior and Repertory Orchestras also participated in domestic exchanges with the Chicago Youth Symphony Orchestras and the Minnesota Youth Symphonies. The BYSO added two new ensembles during the 1990s: the Junior Repertory Orchestra (JRO) and the Preparatory String Orchestra (now known as the Young People's String Orchestra). Other highlights of the decade included children's concerts, a performance with Lynn Chang and Yo-Yo Ma, and the establishment of the Intensive Community Program.

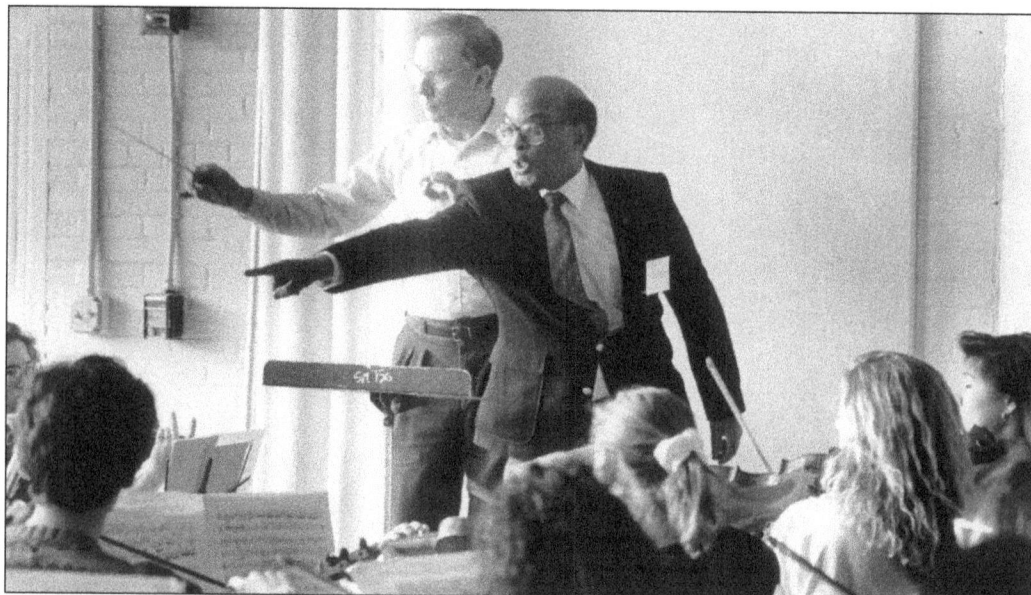

In January 1990, the BYSO and Boston University hosted more than 40 conductors from across the country who attended a three-day workshop sponsored by the American Symphony Orchestra League. Participants conducted the Senior Chamber Orchestra, a string quintet, and a piano ensemble; the repertoire included Antonín Dvořák's *Husitska Overture* and Jean Sibelius's Symphony No. 2. Above, Denis de Coteau (right) works with an aspiring conductor during the workshop.

In 1991, JRO was established. This intermediate-level string ensemble was created in response to a growing need for the training of younger string players. Today JRO includes winds, brass, and percussion, making it a full symphonic orchestra. This image shows JRO with conductor Robert Lehmann during the 1998–1999 season.

On November 23 and 24, 1991, Boston University president Dr. John Silber, shown here with conductor David Commanday, narrated the Senior Orchestra's performance of Sergei Prokofiev's *Peter and the Wolf* at Boston University's Tsai Performance Center. At the end of the program, the musicians invited the young audience onstage to learn about their instruments. This concert was the first in a series of annual concerts for children.

On April 5, 1992, the BYSO presented a concert at Symphony Hall. The Repertory Orchestra, shown here with conductor Joel Bard, opened the program with Edvard Grieg's Three Pieces from *Sigurd Jorsalfar*. The Senior Orchestra then performed *Three Poems of Fiona MacLeod* by Charles Tomlinson Griffes, Samuel Barber's Symphony No. 1, and Josef Suk's Symphony No. 1.

David Commanday led the Senior Orchestra on a tour to central Europe in April 1992. The orchestra performed in four cities during the 10-day trip. The opening concert of the tour took place on April 22 at the Berlin Schauspielhaus, shown here. Wolfgang Schultze, writing for the *Berliner Morgenpost* on April 24, 1992, called the group "an extremely enthusiastic youth orchestra which clearly enjoys playing music and which could serve as an example for some of our comparable orchestras in Germany. Led by the conductor David Commanday, who radiated self-assurance and optimism, the young people offered an imposing performance. They achieved a smashing success." The musicians also presented concerts at Frankfurt's Carl Philipp Emanuel Bach Concert Hall, Prague's Smetana Hall, and Salzburg's Orchesterhaus.

The Senior Orchestra's concert programs during the central European tour were largely made up of music by American composers; the repertory included George Gershwin's *Cuban Overture*, *Three Poems of Fiona MacLeod* by Charles Tomlinson Griffes, Samuel Barber's Symphony No. 1, and Leonard Bernstein's Symphonic Dances from *West Side Story*. Here David Commanday conducts a rehearsal at the Berlin Schauspielhaus.

After visiting Frankfurt and Prague, the Senior Orchestra traveled to Salzburg. Here musicians (from left to right) Valerie Green (class of 1992), Marya Hill-Popper (class of 1992), Jenny Petrow (class of 1992), and Emma Lively (class of 1992) relax with orchestra manager Cathy Cotton during their free time. The final concert of the 1992 tour took place at Salzburg's Orchesterhaus.

Following the 1992 tour to central Europe, the BYSO received its first American Society of Composers, Authors and Publishers Award, given in recognition of the programming of American music on a foreign tour. Senior Orchestra conductor David Commanday traveled to Washington, D.C., to accept the award, which was presented by Morton Gould. Here Commanday conducts the Senior Orchestra at New England Conservatory's Jordan Hall in 1992.

The 1991–1992 season ended with a concert for parents on June 6, 1992, at Harvard University's Sanders Theatre. In his program message, David Commanday wrote, "I am very proud to appear today with this, one of the finest collections of young players GBYSO has known. Our shared experiences in Europe and through long hours of rehearsal this season have resulted in an ensemble spirit and quality which brings me much joy to share with you." Here Tobias Andrews (class of 1993) performs with the Senior Orchestra during a concert in 1992.

Holiday Benefit Concert

Sunday, December 6, 1992
8 p.m.
Symphony Hall, Boston

GREATER
BOSTON
YOUTH
SYMPHONY
ORCHESTRAS

35th Anniversary Season

David Commanday, Music Director

The Senior Orchestra performed at Symphony Hall with the Chicago Youth Symphony Orchestras as a special benefit for the Children's AIDS Program on December 6, 1992; the concert featured Gustav Mahler's Symphony No. 2 ("Resurrection"). The performance was part of the BYSO's 35th anniversary season.

The third annual alumni reunion took place on December 27, 1992, at Boston University. Joel Bard and alumnus David Rahbee (class of 1992) conducted the reunion orchestra, which included more than 50 GBYSO alumni. Harpist Elisabeth Remy (class of 1991), now the principal harpist of the Atlanta Symphony Orchestra, tunes onstage before the orchestra's reading of Symphony No. 4 by Johannes Brahms and Symphony No. 8 by Antonín Dvořák.

In 1991, a consortium consisting of the BYSO, the Interlochen Center for the Arts, the San Francisco Symphony Youth Orchestra, and the Chicago Youth Symphony Orchestra commissioned Olly Wilson (shown here) to write a piece for orchestra. The composition, titled *Expansions III*, received its world premiere at the BYSO's 35th anniversary concert at Symphony Hall on April 4, 1993.

In April 1993, 127 members of the Senior and Repertory Orchestras traveled to Illinois to complete the BYSO's exchange with the Chicago Youth Symphony Orchestras that began earlier that season. The orchestras performed in two concerts and participated in a reading session of Gustav Mahler's Symphony No. 1.

While in Chicago, members of the Senior and Repertory Orchestras enjoyed sightseeing in the city after rehearsals. Pictured from left to right, Susan Hagen (class of 1994), Greta Faulkner (class of 1994), Meredith Grant (class of 1994), and Kristen Noren (class of 1993) pose outside Chicago's Field Museum.

The trip to Chicago included a joint concert at the Chicago Cultural Center, where the Repertory Orchestra played the finale of Alexander Glazunov's Symphony No. 5 and selections from Pyotr Ilich Tchaikovsky's *Swan Lake*. At the final collaborative performance at Chicago's Orchestra Hall (shown here), David Commanday conducted the Senior Orchestra in Samuel Barber's *Third Essay for Orchestra*.

The BYSO presented concerts at the Hatch Memorial Shell on the Charles River Esplanade throughout much of the 1990s. Weather permitting, these concerts brought each season to a close. Above, David Commanday addresses the audience during a performance at the venue with the Senior Orchestra.

In March 1994, David Commanday and the BYSO's Chamber Orchestra performed two educational concerts. The performances featured Joan Bennett Kennedy narrating Sergei Prokofiev's *Peter and the Wolf*, as well as works by Gioachino Rossini, Carl Maria von Weber, and Aaron Copland. Bassoonist Hazy Malcolmson (class of 1995), pictured here, demonstrates her instrument to a group of curious listeners after one of the concerts.

The Greater Boston
Youth Symphony Orchestras
David Commanday, *Music Director*

1994
Scandinavian Tour Kickoff Concert

Friday, April 1, 1994
8 p.m.
Symphony Hall, Boston

GREATER
BOSTON
YOUTH
SYMPHONY
ORCHESTRAS

1994 Scandinavian Tour

In April 1994, the Senior Orchestra traveled to Scandinavia on its 12th international tour. The group performed in five cities in Finland and Sweden, including Turku, Helsinki, Örebro, Göteborg, and Stockholm. At the tour kickoff concert on April 1, 1994, the Senior Orchestra presented pieces that would be performed while overseas.

The 87 members of the Senior Orchestra toured Scandinavia in 1994 with two full programs of music, including *Short Ride on a Fast Machine* by alumnus John Adams (class of 1965), *As Quiet As* by Michael Colgrass, *Appalachian Spring* by Aaron Copland, Concerto for Orchestra by Witold Lutoslawski, Symphony No. 1 by Johannes Brahms, and Concerto for Flute and Orchestra by Carl Nielsen. Boston Symphony Orchestra flutist and GBYSO alumnus Fenwick Smith (class of 1967), shown here with David Commanday at Symphony Hall, joined the orchestra as a soloist for performances at the tour kickoff concert in Boston and at the Konserthuset in Stockholm. Petri Alanko, principal flutist of the Finnish Radio Symphony, performed Nielsen's concerto with the Senior Orchestra in Finland.

The orchestra's first performance of the tour took place at Helsinki's Church in the Rock. The sold-out concert was followed the next day by an afternoon of collaboration with young musicians at Sibelius High School. After riding an ocean liner aptly called the *Symphony* to Stockholm, the orchestra performed in Örebro and Göteborg. David Commanday led the group in a rehearsal at the Göteborg Konserthus, shown here.

The orchestra presented the final concert of the Scandinavian tour on April 25, 1994, at the Stockholm Konserthuset, home of the Royal Philharmonic. The performance included Colgrass's *As Quiet As*, Nielsen's Concerto for Flute and Orchestra, and Brahms's Symphony No. 1.

In April 1994, the Repertory Orchestra, led by conductor Joel Bard, traveled to Minnesota. The orchestra spent one week in St. Paul, which included a concert at St. Catherine's College. The tour was the first part of an exchange with the Minnesota Youth Symphonies' Repertory Orchestra. The following month, the BYSO hosted the Minnesota Youth Symphonies in Boston; members of both orchestras enjoyed a cruise in Boston Harbor.

The Minnesota Youth Symphonies' Repertory Orchestra traveled to Boston for a collaborative concert at Boston University's Tsai Performance Center in May 1994. The program featured "Waltz of the Flowers" from Pyotr Ilich Tchaikovsky's *The Nutcracker Suite*, Modest Petrovich Mussorgsky's *Night on Bald Mountain*, Georges Bizet's Suite No. 1 from *Carmen*, and Dmitri Shostakovich's Symphony No. 5.

In May 1994, the BYSO collaborated with the Boston Ballet II, a program for student dancers, to present *Rumplestiltskin* at Boston University's Tsai Performance Center. The music for the two-act ballet was taken from Bohuslav Martinu's ballet *Spaliček*. Led by David Commanday, the Senior Chamber Orchestra rehearses in the pit in preparation for the production.

During the 1994–1995 season, JRO celebrated its fifth anniversary. In June 1994, David Commanday invited the group to join the Senior Orchestra for a special rehearsal; each JRO musician sat next to an older colleague for a reading of several pieces that JRO had worked on during the season. Above, JRO violinist Christopher Brescia (class of 2002) plays alongside his Senior Orchestra partner Alexia Taylor (class of 1994).

On June 3, 1995, violinist Lynn Chang and cellist Yo-Yo Ma joined David Commanday and the Senior Orchestra in the world premiere of Ivan Tcherepnin's Double Concerto for Violin, Cello, and Orchestra at Harvard University's Sanders Theatre. Commissioned by the BYSO, the 25-minute work, written in three sections joined by "soliloquies" for cello and violin, was the result of nearly three years of planning. Prior to the concert, the Senior Orchestra spent eight weeks practicing the piece, and the soloists joined the group for the final three weeks of rehearsals. The double concerto later won the highly coveted 1996 University of Louisville Grawemeyer Award for Music Composition; GBYSO was the first youth orchestra to be affiliated with this prestigious award. The sold-out concert also included the "Sokol Fanfare" from Leoš Janáček's Sinfonietta and Gustav Mahler's Symphony No. 1. Pictured here from left to right are Lynn Chang, Ivan Tcherepnin, Yo-Yo Ma, and David Commanday.

During the rehearsals leading up to the premiere of Ivan Tcherepnin's piece, Lynn Chang and Yo-Yo Ma frequently offered the members of the Senior Orchestra encouragement and advice. David Commanday often consulted the score with Tcherepnin, then a professor of music at Harvard University, seeking to make the composer's intentions a reality.

The soloists share a light moment during the dress rehearsal at Harvard University's Sanders Theatre. Tcherepnin wrote in his note for the concert program, "I imagined [on the day the work was completed] that I would invite to a celebratory dinner party the composers who had 'participated' in my piece—silent partners whose works made their way into it, sometimes verbatim."

A chamber music group with its coach, alumna Joan Ellersick (class of 1976), takes a break during the 1995 summer music workshop at Agassiz Village in Maine. The BYSO's chamber music program grew significantly in the 1990s; during the 1994–1995 season, 73 students divided into 15 ensembles participated in the program, rehearsing every Sunday morning at Boston University prior to full-orchestra rehearsals.

Established in 1995, the Preparatory String Orchestra, now known as the Young People's String Orchestra (YPSO), was created to train the youngest string players and to prepare them with the skills and techniques necessary to advance into the other BYSO orchestras. This image shows the orchestra with conductor Bonnie Black in the late 1990s.

In November 1995, the Senior Chamber Orchestra presented two children's concerts at Boston University's Tsai Performance Center. Under the direction of David Commanday, the ensemble performed Alberto Ginastera's *Estancia*, five of Aaron Copland's *Old American Songs*, and Sergei Prokofiev's *Peter and the Wolf*. Baritone Stephen Salters joined the orchestra for the Copland songs, and Bruce Marks, artistic director of the Boston Ballet, narrated *Peter and the Wolf*.

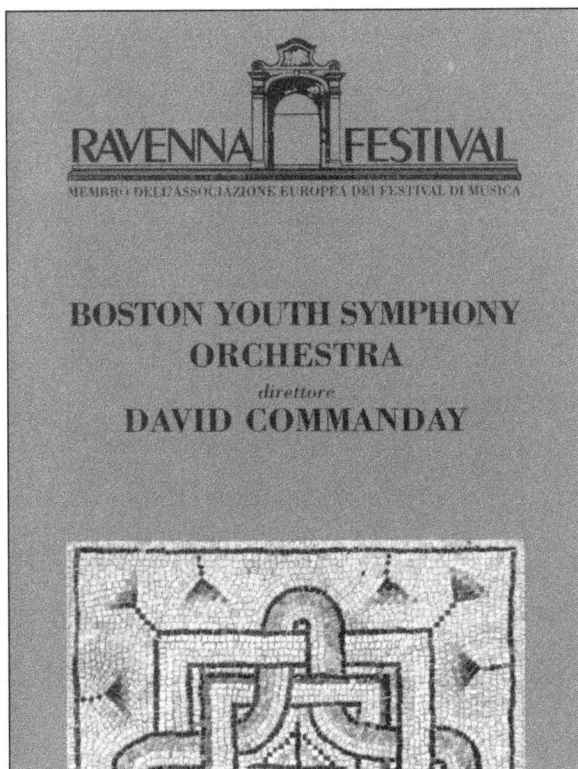

The Senior Orchestra toured Italy in the summer of 1996. The two-week trip, which began on June 22, featured a performance at the renowned Ravenna Festival; the Senior Orchestra was the first youth orchestra to perform at this event. The program featured works by Antonín Dvořák, Prokofiev, Erik Satie, and Leonard Bernstein.

The tour of Italy also included concerts in Reggio Emilia, Como, Florence, Parma, and Rome. At Teatro Sociale in Como, the orchestra performed Sergei Prokofiev's Suite No. 2 from *Romeo and Juliet*, Samuel Barber's Adagio for Strings, Erik Satie's *Gymnopedies No. 1 and 3*, and Leonard Bernstein's Symphonic Dances from *West Side Story*. Many of the venues, such as the one shown here, were outdoors.

In 1997, the BYSO was recognized by National Public Radio's *Performance Today* as one of the nation's five best youth orchestras. Here David Commanday stands in front of the Senior Orchestra at Symphony Hall during the 1996–1997 season.

The program of the BYSO's 40th anniversary gala concert on March 8, 1998, included 20th-century works influenced by African and Latin music. The Repertory Orchestra opened the concert with Morton Gould's *Spirituals*, and the Senior Orchestra continued with Aaron Copland's *Danzón Cubano*, Gould's *Latin-American Symphonette*, and George Gershwin's suite from *Porgy and Bess*.

40th Anniversary Gala "An American Tribute"

David Commanday
Music Director

Sunday
March 8, 1998
Symphony Hall

England & Ireland Tour

David Commanday
Music Director

June 17–July 1, 1998

Birmingham
Aldeburgh
Nottingham
Dublin
Peterborough
Arundel

In the summer of 1998, the Senior Orchestra toured England and Ireland. The orchestra presented concerts at the world-renowned Symphony Hall in Birmingham, the Aldeburgh Festival, the Royal Concert Hall in Nottingham, the National Concert Hall in Dublin, the Peterborough Cathedral Festival, and Arundel Cathedral. During the two-week tour, the 95 members of the Senior Orchestra performed works by Morton Gould, Joseph Schwantner, George Gershwin, Dmitri Kabalevsky, Aaron Copland, Charles Ives, and Igor Stravinsky.

97

The tour of England and Ireland opened on June 19, 1998, with a concert at Symphony Hall in Birmingham. In their free time, members of the Senior Orchestra were able to visit many English landmarks, including Westminster Abbey, Shakespeare's Globe Theatre, and Windsor Castle. After a performance as part of the Aldeburgh Festival and a concert at the Royal Concert Hall in Nottingham, the orchestra traveled to Dublin.

In Dublin, the orchestra performed at the National Concert Hall on June 24, 1998. Ambassador Jean Kennedy Smith honored the students during a reception at the American embassy. The young musicians also visited the Book of Kells at Trinity College and met with members of the Dublin Youth Orchestras and the National Youth Orchestra of Ireland.

During part of the tour, the orchestra members participated in homestays with local families. The last concert of the trip took place at Arundel Cathedral in England; the orchestra performed a program of 20th-century works, including Joseph Schwantner's *Aftertones of Infinity*, Igor Stravinsky's *Firebird Suite,* and George Gershwin's suite from *Porgy and Bess.*

The 1998–1999 season opened with a performance by the Senior Orchestra at the Boston Symphony Orchestra's celebration for Seiji Ozawa's 25th anniversary held on the Boston Common. That year the BYSO was ranked first by the Massachusetts Cultural Council out of 45 grant applicants and was praised as "indistinguishable from an adult orchestra." Here the Repertory Orchestra poses onstage at Symphony Hall during the 1998–1999 season.

Bonnie Black joined the BYSO staff as the conductor of the Preparatory String Orchestra (now known as YPSO) in 1998. The members of this orchestra perform major repertoire from the standard string orchestra literature while learning the skills needed for more advanced orchestral playing. The following year, Black became the artistic director of the BYSO's Intensive Community Program, a rigorous string training program for underrepresented students in classical music. The Intensive Community Program has since become a model arts education program.

Federico Cortese became the music director of the BYSO in 1999. He served as the assistant conductor of the Boston Symphony Orchestra under the direction of Seiji Ozawa from 1998 to 2002. In his first program message, he wrote, "It is so rewarding to make music with such an incredibly talented group of young people! . . . Whether they will decide to become professional musicians or not, music will always be an important part of their lives."

In the summer of 1999, the BYSO began to travel to New England Music Camp in Sidney, Maine, for its annual summer camp. Above, Joel Bard conducts the Repertory Orchestra during the camp-ending concert at New England Music Camp's Bowl in the Pines the following summer.

On November 10, 1999, the Senior and Repertory Orchestras performed at Symphony Hall with guest conductor Keith Lockhart, conductor of the Boston Pops. The program began with Joel Bard leading the Repertory Orchestra in Alexander Borodin's "Polovtsian Dances" from the opera *Prince Igor*. Federico Cortese conducted the Senior Orchestra's performance of Igor Stravinsky's *Petrouchka*, and Keith Lockhart led Antonín Dvořák's Symphony No. 8; the concert marked Cortese's debut performance with the BYSO. During the 1999–2000 season, Cortese initiated the establishment of the Senior Sinfonietta and Senior Camerata, chamber orchestras focused on performing repertoire from the classical period. Here the Senior Orchestra rehearses at Symphony Hall under the direction of Cortese during the 1999–2000 season.

Five

FROM 2000 TO 2007

Since becoming the music director of the BYSO in 1999, Federico Cortese has led the Senior Orchestra on tours of France, central Europe, Estonia, Latvia and Russia, and Spain and Portugal. The BYSO continues to present over 15 concerts each season at some of Boston's finest venues, including Symphony Hall, Harvard University's Sanders Theatre, New England Conservatory's Jordan Hall, and Boston University's Tsai Performance Center. Recent highlights in the BYSO's history include the organization's name change and the 50th anniversary season.

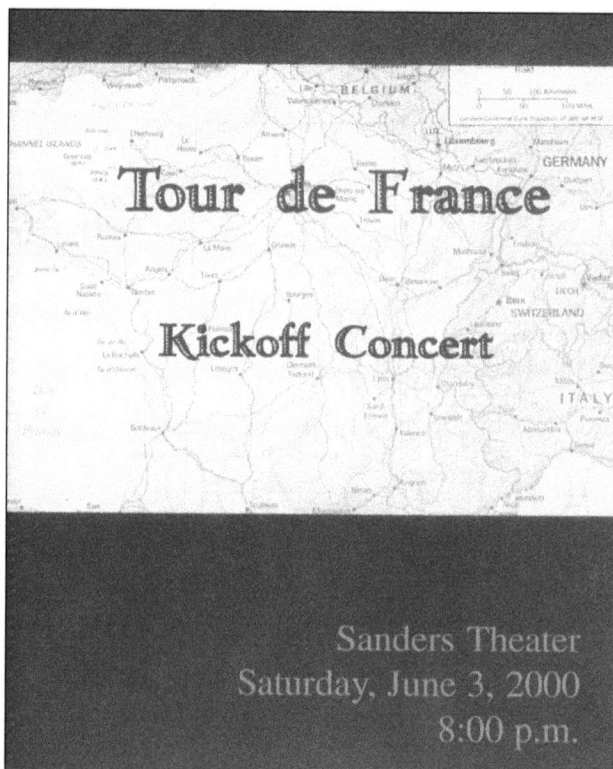

Tour de France

Kickoff Concert

Sanders Theater
Saturday, June 3, 2000
8:00 p.m.

On June 19, 2000, the Senior Orchestra, led by Federico Cortese, traveled to France on its 15th international tour. The kickoff concert, held at Harvard University's Sanders Theatre, featured works by Samuel Barber, George Whitefield Chadwick, Osvaldo Golijov, Leon Kirchner, and Leonard Bernstein. The two-week tour began in Paris, where the orchestra performed at L'Église Saint-Merri as part of La Fête de la Musique.

In Strasbourg, the musicians visited the mayor's mansion (shown here) and performed as part of the prestigious Strasbourg International Music Festival in the Palais de la Musique et des Congrès. From there the orchestra traveled to the heart of the Loire Valley to be featured in the Sully-sur-Loire Festival.

In Provence, the Senior Orchestra performed in Le Val and visited Avignon. The tour continued in Montélimar, where the young musicians participated in the Festival de la Voix et de la Guitare. Orchestra members stayed with host families throughout the trip, which enabled them to meet French students and experience French culture. Finally the orchestra presented a concert as part of the Printemps Musicale in Roanne before returning to Boston on July 2, 2000.

Two of the BYSO's ensembles performed at Symphony Hall on October 15, 2000, during the venue's centennial celebration. Joel Bard conducted the Repertory Orchestra in Antonín Dvořák's *The Golden Spinning Wheel*, and Federico Cortese led the Senior Orchestra in Pyotr Ilich Tchaikovsky's *Francesca da Rimini*. Pictured here, members of the Senior Orchestra perform at Symphony Hall earlier that year.

During the 2000–2001 season, the Senior Orchestra traveled to Chicago to perform in an exchange concert with the Chicago Youth Symphony Orchestras. BYSO students stayed with host families and toured the city, visiting the Field Museum and the Art Institute of Chicago. The two orchestras performed at Northwestern University's Pick Staiger Hall. The Chicago Youth Symphony Orchestras opened the concert with Igor Stravinsky's Suite No. 1 for Small Orchestra and Wolfgang Amadeus Mozart's Symphony No. 40; the Senior Orchestra then performed Maurice Ravel's *Pavane pour une infante défunte* and Ludwig van Beethoven's Symphony No. 2. The Chicago Youth Symphony Orchestras completed the exchange by traveling to Boston to perform in a joint program at the Isabella Stewart Gardner Museum on April 21, 2001. The 2000–2001 Senior Orchestra season also included two performances at Boston's Symphony Hall (shown above).

On February 3, 2002, Sinfonietta and Camerata, chamber orchestras composed of Senior Orchestra members, performed an all-Mozart program at Harvard University's Sanders Theatre. The Senior Orchestra assistant conductor Mark Miller led Camerata in Mozart's Symphony No. 31 ("Paris"), and soloists from the Boston University Opera Institute joined Federico Cortese and Sinfonietta to perform Act I of Mozart's *Cosi fan tutte*. From left to right, Peter Ajemian (class of 2002), Wynton McCurdy (class of 2004), and Nicholas Jemo (class of 2002) perform at Symphony Hall during the 2001–2002 season.

On March 10, 2002, the Senior Orchestra performed *Ein deutches requiem* by Johannes Brahms with the Tanglewood Festival Chorus at Symphony Hall; this concert marked the BYSO's first collaboration with the official chorus of the Boston Symphony Orchestra. The Senior Orchestra's repertoire that season also included Pyotr Ilich Tchaikovsky's Symphony No. 4, Franz Liszt's *Les Préludes*, Zoltán Kodály's *Dances of Galanta*, and Béla Bartók's Suite from *The Miraculous Mandarin*.

On June 23, 2002, 91 members of the Senior Orchestra departed on a tour of central Europe. The trip included concerts in four cities in the Czech Republic, Poland, and Hungary. In Prague, the orchestra explored the Old City district before presenting the first concert, which took place at Dvořák Hall in the Rudolfinum on June 26, 2002. The following day, the orchestra departed by bus for Kraków, Poland.

On June 29, 2002, the Senior Orchestra performed Leonard Bernstein's Overture to *Candide*, Zoltán Kodály's *Dances of Galanta*, and Pyotr Ilich Tchaikovsky's Symphony No. 4 at Filharmonia Hall in Kraków. In Poland, the orchestra visited the Wielicza Salt Mines, as well as Kraków's Old Town historic district.

In Debrecen, Hungary, the Senior Orchestra joined the opening festivities of the 20th biannual Béla Bartók Choir Competition, performing in Béla Bartók Hall on July 2, 2002. The program included Bernstein's Overture to *Candide* and Bartók's Suite from *The Miraculous Mandarin*.

A performance at Vigado Concert Hall in Budapest (shown here) and a farewell cruise on the Danube River marked the conclusion of the BYSO's 16th international tour.

During the 2002–2003 season, JRO became a full symphonic orchestra with wind, brass, and percussion players; up until this time, JRO had been an ensemble exclusively for strings. In addition to this expansion, JRO musicians began participating in sight-singing and ear-training lessons instituted to create a solid musical foundation for students as they move up through the orchestras. Pictured here is cellist Kevin Lee (class of 2007) in 2003.

The BYSO's 45th anniversary during the 2002–2003 season featured concerts at Symphony Hall, Harvard University's Sanders Theatre, Boston University's Tsai Performance Center, and the Hatch Memorial Shell on the Charles River Esplanade. Federico Cortese's fourth season as the BYSO's music director included performances of works by Igor Stravinsky, Antonín Dvořák, Richard Strauss, Benjamin Britten, and Maurice Ravel, as well as a collaboration with the Boston University Opera Programs to present Act II of Wolfgang Amadeus Mozart's *Le nozze di Figaro.*

On March 31, 2003, the Preparatory String Orchestra and the Intensive Community Program Orchestra, led by conductor Bonnie Black, performed at Symphony Hall as part of the annual Classical Cartoon Festival. Here the young musicians rehearse onstage before the concert.

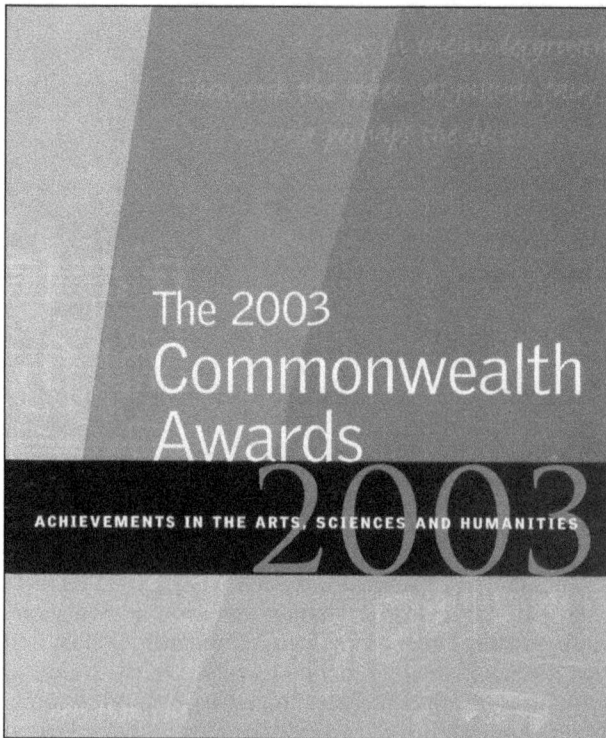

The 2003
Commonwealth
Awards
2003
ACHIEVEMENTS IN THE ARTS, SCIENCES AND HUMANITIES

In March 2003, the Massachusetts Cultural Council awarded the BYSO the prestigious Commonwealth Award in the education category, given every two years as the state's highest recognition for individuals and organizations in the arts, humanities, and interpretive sciences. With this award, the council recognized the BYSO as a model program and outstanding contributor to the advancement of excellence in the arts.

In June 2003, the Senior Orchestra toured California. During the five-day trip, the orchestra performed in Napa Valley at a benefit concert for the newly formed Napa Valley Youth Symphony and at the Mondavi Center at the University of California in Davis. The repertoire for the tour included Nikolai Rimsky-Korsakov's *Scheherazade*, Igor Stravinsky's Symphony in Three Movements, and Ludwig van Beethoven's Symphony No. 8. From left to right, Shailey DeVito (class of 2006), Emi Ferguson (class of 2005), Will Fryer (class of 2004), and Camille White (class of 2004) perform at Symphony Hall during the 2003–2004 season.

On November 16, 2003, the Senior and Repertory Orchestras performed at Symphony Hall (shown here). Joel Bard and the Repertory Orchestra opened the concert with César Franck's *Le chasseur maudit*, and Federico Cortese led the Senior Orchestra in Igor Stravinsky's *Le chant du rossignol* and Symphonic Excerpts from Hector Berlioz's *Roméo et Juliette*. Later that season, the Sinfonietta and Camerata chamber orchestras performed an all-Mozart program at Harvard University's Sanders Theatre, including Symphony No. 39 and selections from the opera *Don Giovanni*. The spring concert at Symphony Hall on March 14, 2004, featured Sergei Prokofiev's *Overture Russe*, Jean Sibelius's Symphony No. 3, and Prokofiev's *Alexander Nevsky Cantata*; Chorus pro Musica, directed by Jeffrey Rink, joined the Senior Orchestra for the final Prokofiev work.

During the 2003–2004 season, the Repertory Orchestra performed challenging works by Ludwig van Beethoven, Henryk Wieniawski, and Alexander Borodin. On May 2, 2004, the orchestra presented a concert at Boston University's Tsai Performance Center; the program featured Maurice Ravel's Suite of Five Pieces from *Mother Goose*, and Antonín Dvořák's Symphony No. 6. That season, performances by JRO, the Preparatory String Orchestra, and the Intensive Community Program Orchestra included pieces by Edvard Grieg, Aaron Copland, and Johann Pachelbel. Pictured here are violinists Samantha Velasquez and Roland Bai Liu.

In the summer of 2004, members of the Senior Orchestra departed on the BYSO's 17th international tour to Estonia, Latvia, and Russia. Shown here in St. Petersburg, 95 students performed four concerts in Tallinn, Riga, St. Petersburg, and Novgorod. The repertoire for the trip included Osvaldo Golijov's *Night of the Flying Horses*, Igor Stravinsky's *Le chant du rossignol*, Johannes Brahms's Symphony No. 3, and Symphonic Excerpts from Hector Berlioz's *Roméo et Juliette*.

In Estonia's capital city of Tallinn, the Senior Orchestra performed at the Estonia Concert Hall and toured the city's Old Town. From Estonia, the group traveled to Riga, Latvia, where the orchestra presented a concert in the assembly hall of the Blackheads House, a medieval building that once housed guards who protected the city. Above, percussionists (from left to right) Maddie Child (class of 2004), Sam Dent (class of 2004), John Beder (class of 2004), and Gabe Globus-Hoenich (class of 2004) warm up backstage before a concert.

The musicians traveled on an overnight train from Riga to St. Petersburg, where they performed at the world-renowned Shostakovich Hall (pictured here). In Russia, the orchestra enjoyed a guided tour of the city, as well as visits to the Hermitage Museum and Peterhof, the summer residence of Peter the Great.

The orchestra performed Osvaldo Golijov's *Night of the Flying Horses*, Igor Stravinsky's *La Chant du rossignol*, and Hector Berlioz's Symphonic Excerpts from *Roméo et Juliette* in the historic Shostakovich Hall (shown here) on July 1, 2004. The performance garnered a standing ovation from the sold-out house. The final concert of the tour took place in Novgorod, one of the most ancient cities in Russia. After playing at Novgorod Philharmonic Hall, the orchestra members spent their last evening together on a farewell dinner cruise in St. Petersburg on the Neva River.

GREATER BOSTON
Youth Symphony
Orchestras

Federico Cortese • Music Director

On April 10, 2005, the Senior Orchestra presented Giuseppe Verdi's *Messa da requiem* at Boston's Symphony Hall with Chorus pro Musica, one of New England's leading choral ensembles. The performance featured soprano Indra Thomas, mezzo-soprano Eleni Matos, tenor Philip Webb, and bass Stephen Morscheck. The concert opened with the Repertory Orchestra's performance of Béla Bartók's Four Orchestral Pieces. The season finale concert on June 12, 2005, at New England Conservatory's Jordan Hall included works by Michael Tippett, Pablo Sarasate, Johann Sebastian Bach, Anton Webern, and Ludwig van Beethoven.

During the 2005–2006 season, the Repertory Orchestra was split for the first time into two chamber orchestras. The Repertory Sinfonietta and Repertory Camerata focus on performing music from the classical period, allowing students the unique opportunity to master the difficult stylistic nuances of this period. Here bassist Ifeanyi Chukwujama performs with the Repertory Orchestra during a concert at Symphony Hall on November 20, 2005.

On November 20, 2005, the Senior and Repertory Orchestras performed at Symphony Hall. Joel Bard and the Repertory Orchestra opened the concert with Léo Delibes's Suite No. 2 from Coppélia, and the Senior Orchestra followed with Gioachino Rossini's Overture to Semiramide, Igor Stravinsky's The Fairy's Kiss: Divertimento, and Antonín Dvořák's Symphony No. 7.

On December 11, 2005, the Intensive Community Program Orchestra, led by Bonnie Black, performed a holiday concert "by children, for children" that included works by George Frideric Handel, Felix Mendelssohn, and Pyotr Ilich Tchaikovsky. The Boston Children's Chorus joined the Intensive Community Program Orchestra at the end of the concert to perform "Let it Snow," "Winter Wonderland," and other holiday songs.

GREATER
Boston Youth Symphony
ORCHESTRAS

49TH SEASON

Holiday Concert
By Children, For Children

Intensive Community
Program Orchestra

Bonnie Black
Artistic Director

with special guests
Boston Children's Chorus
Anthony Trecek-King, *Artistic Director*

Presented in collaboration with
Roxbury Community College

December 10, 2006
6:00pm

On January 29, 2006, the BYSO's Sinfonietta and Camerata chamber orchestras performed at Harvard University's Sanders Theatre with Chorus pro Musica. The concert opened with Federico Cortese conducting Wolfgang Amadeus Mozart's *La clemenza di Tito* and Mozart's Symphony No. 38 ("Prague"). Assistant conductor Mark Miller then led Camerata in Franz Joseph Haydn's Mass in D minor ("Lord Nelson").

In June 2006, the Senior Orchestra toured Spain and Portugal. On June 20, 101 musicians departed for a 12-day trip including four concerts. In Portugal, the orchestra journeyed to the picturesque seaside towns of Sintra and Cascais and took a walking tour of Lisbon's castle district. The first concert at the Centro Culturel de Belém featured Gustav Mahler's Symphony No. 4 with soprano Theresa Gardner.

From Lisbon, the group traveled by bus to Spain. The orchestra members explored Seville's maze of narrow streets and visited the famous mosque at Cordoba. On June 26, 2006, the Senior Orchestra presented a concert at the University of Seville. The program featured Gioachino Rossini's Overture to *Semiramide*, Igor Stravinsky's *The Fairy's Kiss*: Divertimento, and Antonín Dvořák's Symphony No. 7.

In Granada, the Senior Orchestra visited Alhambra Palace and attended a flamenco dancing show in the Albayzin district. For many students, the concert in Granada was the highlight of the tour. The orchestra took part in the prestigious Granada Festival, and hundreds gathered to watch the dress rehearsal and concert at the Plaza de las Pasiegas. Shouts of "bravo" filled the streets at the conclusion of the program's final piece, Dvořák's Symphony No. 7.

The orchestra traveled by overnight train from Granada to Barcelona, where the musicians visited the 1992 Olympic complex and Antoni Gaudi's famous Holy Family Cathedral. The final concert of the tour took place on July 1, 2006, at the new Auditori Enric Granados in the town of Lleida, outside Barcelona. Here the orchestra rehearses for the last time onstage before the performance.

At the beginning of the 2006–2007 season, the BYSO expanded its summer program at the New England Music Camp from one to two weeks. As a result of this extended commitment at camp, the Senior Orchestra's concert schedule was broadened to include five full programs of repertoire, the most extensive concert schedule of any youth orchestra in the United States.

The Preparatory String Orchestra, conducted by Bonnie Black, became known as YPSO at the beginning of the 2006–2007 season to reflect more accurately the advanced nature of the BYSO's youngest string ensemble. Since its inception in 1995, YPSO has become known as one of the finest children's orchestras in New England.

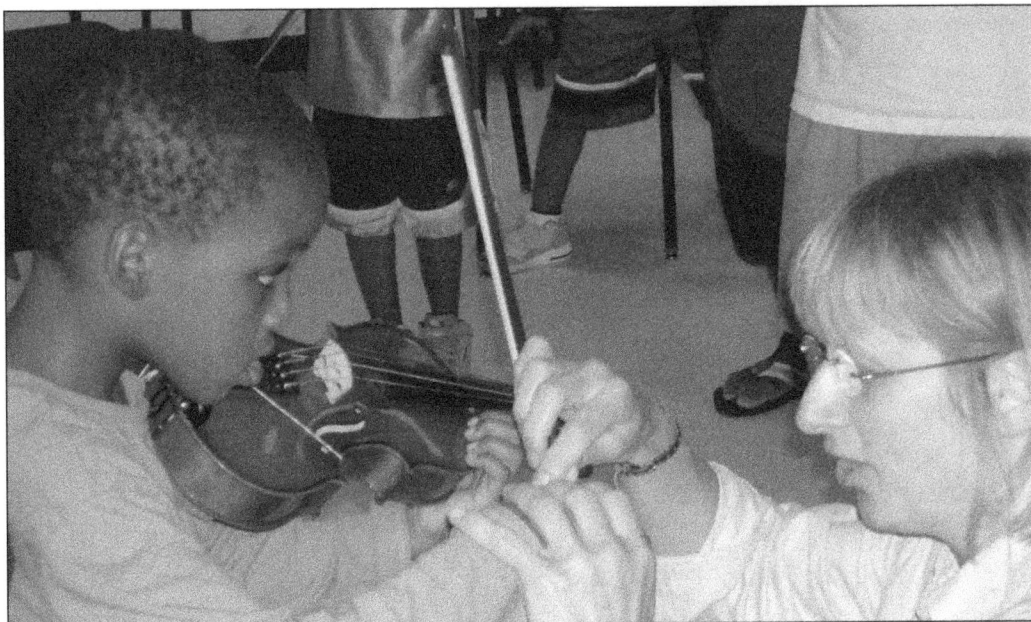

The Intensive Community Program, led by Bonnie Black, grew dramatically between 2000 and 2006; by the 2006–2007 season, enrollment in the program had increased to 77 students, 31 of which were members of the BYSO orchestras. Prior to the establishment of Intensive Community Program, only 1 percent of BYSO students were drawn from inner-city Boston communities. In 2007, 20 percent of the BYSO's student body came from these communities.

In 2006, the Preparatory Wind Ensemble was created to teach young wind players the fundamental skills necessary for successful orchestral playing. Under the direction of Janet Underhill, members of the Preparatory Wind Ensemble develop basic techniques for ensemble participation that help prepare them for future orchestra membership. During the 2006–2007 season, the ensemble was comprised of 18 middle school–age musicians from Massachusetts and New Hampshire.

On March 12, 2007, the Greater Boston Youth Symphony Orchestras officially changed its name to the Boston Youth Symphony Orchestras. On that day, the Senior Orchestra became known as the Boston Youth Symphony. Above, Nathaniel Meyer and his sister Rebekah (class of 2007) warm up backstage at Symphony Hall during the 2006–2007 season.

The first BYSO concert under the organization's new name took place on April 22, 2007, at Symphony Hall. The Boston Youth Symphony performed Igor Stravinsky's *Jeu de cartes* and Symphony No. 1 by Johannes Brahms. Bonnie Black also led YPSO and members of the Intensive Community Program in Jean Sibelius's *Andante festivo*, the March and Reprise from Ralph Vaughn Williams's Concerto Grosso for Strings, Georges Bizet's "Toreador Song" from *Carmen*, and Catherine McMichael's *Pax*.

The concert on April 22, 2007, marked the first time that the Boston Youth Symphony and YPSO had performed on the same stage. In an effort to better present the scope of the BYSO's program, the concert schedule was restructured so that each of the four orchestras and the Preparatory Wind Ensemble would have the opportunity to perform together during the season.

The 2007–2008 season marks the BYSO's 50th anniversary; in the first half century of its history, the BYSO has served thousands of young musicians from throughout New England and presented concerts in venues in North America, Europe, Asia, South America, and the Middle East. Although the BYSO has transformed dramatically since its inception in 1958, the values instilled in the organization since its founding remain intact today. Nationally recognized as a model music and arts education organization, the BYSO serves the community by encouraging a greater understanding of and participation in classical music.

PHOTOGRAPH CREDITS

Barstow, John, 122 bottom, 124 top
Bassett, Betsy, 101 top
Bodin, Fredrik, 31 top, 51 bottom, 52 top and bottom, 53 bottom, 54 top and bottom, 55 bottom, 56, 58 top and bottom, 59 top, 60, 64 bottom, 70
Boris and Milton, 9, 11 top, 12 bottom, 13, 16 top, 17 bottom, 18, 19 top and bottom, 26 top, 29 top
Boston University Photo Services, 10 bottom, 12 top, 15 top, 16 bottom, 21 bottom, 22 top, 23 top, 27 bottom, 28 top and bottom, 35, 37, 40 bottom, 41 bottom, 79 top, 84 top, 87 top, 88, 91 top and bottom, 93 top
Chapman, Kathy, 74 top and bottom
Cohen, Dana, 43 top and bottom, 44 top
Covert, Diane, 96 bottom, 110 bottom, 114 top
Ed Kirwan Graphic Arts, 84 bottom
Ellersick, Joan, 46
Herzog, Bradford, 61 bottom, 69 bottom, 76
Hires, Ben, 123 bottom
Le Cault, Larry, 123 top
Lutch, Michael, 2, 106, 107 top and bottom, 112 bottom, 118 top and bottom, 119 bottom, 124 bottom, 125 top and bottom, 126
Mosher, James, 49 bottom
Nessikian, Felix, 30 top
Pelissier, Roger, 75 top, 92
Rosenthal, Karin, 55 top
Swienink-Havard, Marianne, 120 top, 121, 122 top
Tanzer, Christian, 79 bottom
Terry's Photography, 85 top, 86 top
Vintoniv, Miro, 93 bottom
Wiles, Christopher, 17 top

Visit us at
arcadiapublishing.com

www.ingramcontent.com/pod-product-compliance
Lightning Source LLC
Chambersburg PA
CBHW080601110426
42813CB00006B/1370